No. 13, Bob

John Cooper

Captain Starr

JEAN OVERTON FULLER

No. 13, Bob

Little, Brown and Company • Boston • Toronto

FOR
MICHELLE

Author's Note

Book i of this story is written practically as it was told me by Captain Starr. I have even kept the same phrases as far as possible, so that I should not come between him and the reader any more than I could help. As regards the important Avenue Foch chapters, while I have been very careful not to include any incidents about which Captain Starr's memory is not absolutely sure, he does not know their dates; and while he has tried to allocate them approximately to the right time of year, he cannot vouch even for the order in which they happened.

The whole book was read by Captain Starr before publication.

Jean Overton Fuller

Contents

BOOK ONE
Starr's Story

I

An Artist Joins the Army

HE HAD SOME difficulty in getting into a service. By
profession he was a poster artist and, after studying as a
boy in France, he made his home there, married a
Frenchwoman, and settled down in a suburb of Paris.
His name was John Starr.

Eight months before war was declared in 1939, he
went to the office of the Military Attaché in Paris and
volunteered for the R.A.F. in the event of war. In August he, his wife Michelle and their little daughter were
holidaying on the Côte d'Azur, and September 3 found
them at a small seaside town near Cannes. They left
immediately and arrived in Paris the following night.
Early next morning Starr reported, as he had been instructed when he volunteered, to the offices of the R.A.F.
To his fury, he was told that he could not be accepted
because, although a British subject himself, his father
was an American — a fact which had not mattered before. Now the personnel had changed, and it did.

He haunted the R.A.F. offices, hoping to be accepted
in spite of his father, until the spring of 1940, when an
officer came over to Paris to recruit for the Army. With
great difficulty, Starr persuaded the Army to take him,

his American father again proving a hurdle which was only surmounted after special permission had been obtained from the War Office. There would probably be a job for him, he was told, though for the time being its nature could not be revealed. He need not go to England for training (this had at one time been threatened, but Starr had protested, for he had done some years in the Officers' Training Corps and it seemed futile to send him back to England when a large part of the British Army was already in the field in France), but he would have to do ten days with the King's Own Scottish Borderers, who were stationed at Rouen.

It was during this training that he learned his destiny — the Field Security Police, at that time a branch of the Military Police which was destined to be incorporated into the Intelligence Corps when it was formed.

His training took place during the period when the Germans had begun to break through, and columns of soldiers mingled with refugees, retreating regiments, lorries, tanks, guns and pathetic little groups of people carrying with them whatever possessions they could. Starr knew the roads around Rouen well, for his parents-in-law lived close by; and it was a shock to him to see the peaceful countryside filled with the scars of war as the Germans advanced with ever greater rapidity.

After the ten days' training — a somewhat farcical training in the circumstances — he reported to the Field Security Police section at Nantes, where he found the other men who had been destined for it. Here instructions were given them in the duties of the F.S.P.: to keep their eyes open for anything suspicious, to investigate reports that might come in of anything peculiar — in short, to protect the Army by acting as counterespionage agents in the field.

As the section was very shorthanded and overworked, after only a few classes they were detailed to go out on real jobs. But their work at Nantes was soon brought to an end by *force majeure* — the advance of the Germans — and Starr found himself heading at full speed for St. Nazaire on a motor bike (he had ridden one only twice before in the course of his training). With his companions he embarked for Plymouth, which they reached after four days and nights, zigzagging all the way. At Plymouth they were given four days' leave, and at the end of this period they were to report to the F.S.P. training center at King Alfred's College, Winchester.

That afternoon Starr left for Newcastle-under-Lyme, Staffordshire, where his wife and child (whom he had sent to England some months before) were staying with his parents. It was a very relieved family that welcomed him home. They were growing anxious, as his brother George — later to play a gallant part in underground work in occupied France — had already been back some time.

When Starr arrived at Winchester after his brief leave, he found that he and the colleagues who had come back from France with him had to start again from scratch, despite their recent service in the field. For several weeks they were not even allowed to begin training, but were given all the fatigues — dish-washing, road-mending, trench-digging and the rest of it. This by no means suited their book; but since they had all volunteered overseas (which caused them to be known as the "Foreign Legion") they came to the conclusion that the authorities were finding out who they were before allowing them to start proper training.

Starr himself had a piece of luck, for it was discovered that "in real life" he was a poster artist, and from that time onwards he never saw a potato or a shovel as long as he was in the Army — he was kept far too busy designing posters of various kinds. In time he was promoted to drawing portraits of the officers, and at one point even found himself installed for this purpose in a room at the War Office. It seemed to him a strange situation that a lance corporal should be ensconced here, while generals and other high-ranking officers would knock on the door, asking diffidently if he was ready for them — to which the lance corporal would often reply, "I'm sorry, sir, but you'll have to wait a minute. I'll let you know when you can come in."

After many months had passed like this — the designing of a recognition poster for the Home Office being the only job of any real value — Starr, who had been promised important work, got very impatient with waiting so long and so fruitlessly and despite frequent protests to his superior officers. So he made a formal application in writing, and shortly afterwards was called to the colonel's office.

"I believe you speak French fluently, don't you?" the colonel asked.

"Yes, sir. Not only do I speak French very well; I believe that I also *know* the French very well."

"In that case, would you like to go to France?"

Starr jumped at this, and there and then an appointment was made for him to have an interview in London. When the time for it came he asked the officer who interviewed him whether there might not be an opening in propaganda work in France, as that was something in his line.

"You would have to do a certain amount of training first," came the reply. "You needn't worry about the problem of getting there — we have our means. But have you thought this matter over thoroughly? Do you know what you are risking? If you are captured by the enemy you will be shot."

"Yes, I quite realize that," said Starr. "But I'd like to try for the job."

"Very well. Wait four days and write to me then if you still want to go."

"I don't have to wait four days. I've already decided."

But the officer insisted on the delay, so it was not until four days later that Starr was able to send the letter. At very short notice after that he left Oxford, where he was then stationed, for "an unknown destination."

Not very long before, he had told Michelle what he

was doing. She was very upset, and said, "But it's so terribly dangerous! You may never come back. Why did
you have to volunteer for a thing like this?" But when
she realized that his mind was made up, she said, "In
that case, I should like a son to remember you by."

Starr returned to London and reported for the first
time to an office in Orchard Court which has since been
much written about. So began his career with the French
Section of S.O.E. Special Operations Executive, to give
it its full title, was an organization created during the
war which sent out agents to work secretly in countries
occupied by the Germans. It was divided into a "French
Section," a "Dutch Section," a "Norwegian Section,"and
so on, and was a purely British organization. Its work
was twofold: sabotage and the destruction of machinery
of all kinds — plants, power stations, mines, locks, rail-
ways — on the one hand; and, on the other, the secret
arming and organization of local patriots so that they
should be able, when the Allied invasion took place, to
rise at a signal and play a part in the liberation of their
homelands.

It was not an espionage organization; and (in the
French Section at any rate) agents who were sent over
were told that if captured they should, for their own
protection, tell the Germans their ranks as officers, in
the hope that, although they were not in uniform, their
captors might feel disposed to treat them as prisoners of
war and not as spies.

At Orchard Court, Starr found also the men who were

to become his companions in training, and that same day they set out for Wanborough Manor, in Surrey, where they were to begin their training.

Starr, who at this time knew neither the nature of S.O.E. nor that he was destined for it, but still had in mind that he was going to do some propaganda work, was naturally somewhat surprised when an officer began a course on the use of explosives. There were about fourteen of them on this course. Among them was a man called Rabinovitch, afterwards "Arnaud," who was on it with Starr from the beginning, though he cannot be certain if they belonged to the same group right through. They were later to meet in France. Two others taking the course who were to play a part in his story were Alfred and Henry Newton, brothers who had lost their entire family in the war; they were rather placed under Starr's wing.

Apart from physical training, and such courses as the use of arms and explosives, the men were sent out on various "schemes" to test their resource. Once they were briefed to a certain English town, to gather all possible information about the disposition of troops stationed there and other matters, and to put in a report on their return. The Intelligence Corps were in the game, and had been briefed to watch out for them and obstruct them in the performance of their duty. Starr had an adventurous day, for he was spotted by a man from the Intelligence Corps, whom he kept at bay by a brilliant piece of bluffing, and he finished by being taken to the police station with the threat of interrogation at Divisional Headquarters. However, he managed to escape, and landed back at Wanborough Manor with all the information he was supposed to obtain. He was commissioned immediately for his success in this job.

After further training, including a toughening-up course of the commando type, Starr was sent to a school in the New Forest for a course in security. His work here included the "sabotaging," with six others, of the Manchester Ship Canal, a tricky job which needed a great deal of thought, skill and planning. They carried it out, however, with complete success, and won high commendation.

Eventually, after further courses, Starr found himself back in London. He still had in mind that he was ultimately destined for propaganda, and asked where all this was leading to. "The time has passed for propaganda," he was told.

Then one day, when he reported at Orchard Court, he was told, "You're the food expert."

"I'm the *what*?"

"You're the food expert." The officer who had broken this news went on to explain that a certain chief of the French Resistance had asked London to send them a food expert.

"But I know nothing about it!"

"Well, we've got three days to teach you."

He was shown round the meat market and other

places, and tried to store in his memory as much as he could of what he gathered.

Just before leaving he said, "I still don't get it. I still don't know enough about it. It would take much longer than three days to know anything worth while about it. Why have I been chosen for this job?"

"Because there's nobody available to send, and we were pretty certain that you'd be able to bluff the French that you were a food expert, or anything else!"

He thought this was rather a curious way of helping the French Resistance, which to his mind was a very serious matter, but said nothing more about it. He was told that he would go to France almost immediately, and that his code name would be "Emile."

Thinking about it afterwards, he was thankful that although a greenhorn, he nevertheless managed to be useful in the curious métier that had been thrust upon him.

11
"Food Expert"

IT WAS AT THE time of the August full moon, in 1942, that he was parachuted for the first time into France. He was dropped "blind" — that is to say, with no reception committee waiting on the ground to meet him — over a field near Valence chosen in London; only, as he fell rushing down, he saw coming up to meet him not the field, but trees and a farmstead. He passed through the top of a poplar tree, and then through a fruit tree, and the branches took off the first-aid package on his leg. Then he bumped up against the wall of the farmhouse.

His first duty was to bury the parachute, and he took the spade attached to the suitcase which had come down with him. In England they had been taught how to remove a layer of earth intact, and then, after burying the parachute, put the soil back again so carefully that the patch would not be noticeable. However, he found the sun-baked earth of the South of France so hard that he could hardly make any impression on it. After jabbing about for some time without adequate results, he gave up and simply laid the parachute out on the edge of a plowed field, and then shoveled some of the loosened earth on top of it. His overall and rubber helmet he hid underneath a hedge.

Next he went to look for the second parachute, which had brought down the food that was to last until he should obtain food tickets. When he found it he realized that the cargo had been made up in the form of one huge crate which, fit as he was, he was unable to lift. So he dragged it, with great effort, to a haystack, pushed it in and pulled some of the hay on top of it. Then he disposed of the second parachute in the same way as the first.

He threw away his revolver, as it would be dangerous to have it found on him, and started to walk to Valence, about eighteen kilometers away. He had been instructed to avoid buildings of any kind until he got right away from the scene of the parachute operation, but as he was getting very tired he risked passing through one small village, rather than make a cumbersome detour. Inevitably the dogs started barking. He thought it best to do what any normal inhabitant of France would have done, and cursed them loudly.

Shortly after this he met the first person he had encountered in France, an old woman coming along the pathway. To his relief, she took no notice of him. Then, just before he got to Valence, he stopped by a stream for a wash, shave and brush-up, and went on into the town.

He realized just in time that he was about to make the mistake of going into the town before the inhabitants were astir, for there was hardly anybody in the streets.

So he went out again and hid in the garden of an abandoned house. He was rather puzzled that there had been so few people about, as it wasn't particularly early. On his second attempt the streets were more populous, and he went into a café. Here he noticed that the clock was an hour behind his watch; and suddenly it flashed on him that French time was one hour earlier than British summer time — that was the explanation of the empty streets.

As he knew that there were certain things which were sold only on certain days, and had not yet found out what they were, he dared not order an *apéritif* or coffee or tea or anything that might be rationed, but he thought he could risk asking for a lemonade. This came without difficulty.

After that he made his way to the station, joined in a crowd of people and took a ticket to Marseilles. His destination was really Cannes, but he thought it better to break the journey and take a second ticket.

At one of the stations a lady got in with a lot of luggage and a baby. He helped her to put her cases on the rack, and she said, "*Merci beaucoup, monsieur.*" He was horrified to hear himself reply in English, "That's quite all right." Luckily, nobody seemed to notice.

Towards lunchtime a French family, mother, father and child, opened up a case and brought out a pathetic-looking piece of bread and an apple. Starr had chicken in both his pockets, which he had brought from England and which he had been meaning to take out and eat as soon as it got late enough not to appear an odd time for lunch. But now, watching this French family having their very thin meal, he felt that he could not take the chicken out of his pockets and eat it in front of them.

He was, however, becoming more and more desperately hungry, and in the end he went along to the toilet, meaning to have his chicken there. But when he unwrapped it, he found it was so "high" as to be uneatable. There was nothing to do except put it down the lavatory and pull the plug.

At Marseilles he got out, had some more lemonade and took a further ticket to Cannes. When he got out of the train, he tacked himself on to a large family, in order not to be conspicuous as a solitary traveler.

He had now to report to a villa some way out of the town. He was so tired that he could not resist taking a velo-taxi (a bicycle arrangement pulling a basket chair on wheels), telling the driver that he didn't remember the number of the house, but would recognize it when he saw it. He let the man go some way past the place, then stopped him and walked back when the velo-taxi had disappeared. There was someone in the garden, by the door, and supposing that this must be his "contact," he said his password. To his dismay, he got no answer. Then he realized that this was only the concierge's lodge, of which he had not been told, and that the villa lay behind. He asked after the man whom he had come to see.

"He's out," said the concierge.

"But I'm expected," said Starr, puzzled.

"He's out," repeated the concierge.

"D'you mind if I go up?"

The concierge made no objections, but there was obviously nobody in. Starr waited some hours, until about midnight he saw the glow of a cigarette coming along the path. At once he said the password.

The answer which he got — in English — was, "What the hell are you doing here?"

Then another cigarette appeared, and when the face behind this one became visible Starr recognized a major of S.O.E. with whom he had spoken only a few days before he left London.

Starr said, with very genuine feeling, how pleased he was to see him.

They asked him again how on earth he had gotten there. "We were waiting at the station, and we'd ordered a fine black-market meal for you, but we didn't see you. We watched all the people getting out of the train."

He had hidden himself in the large French family too successfully.

Assuring him that they could scratch up a meal, they took him into the splendid villa and up to a lovely bedroom with a private bathroom attached.

As it was the height of summer, the people who had been living on the Côte d'Azur for any time were all burned brown. So as not to be conspicuously a new arrival, he spent the next two or three days sunbathing in the garden, to turn the right color as quickly as possible, while somebody got him clothes appropriate to a beach-lounging kind of life.

When he looked more natural they took him to the agreed rendezvous at the Casino Theater in Cannes and introduced him to the chief of the French Resistance of the area during a rehearsal of *Poil de Carotte*. The chief had chosen this place for the rendezvous because his daughter, Danielle Délorme, now one of the leading actresses in France, was playing the title role. This was the man whom he had to bluff that he was a food expert — not altogether a comfortable job. His mission was the organization of a sort of relief food service throughout the country so that any isolated Resistance group could be fed.

Afterwards he was taken to Antibes and given a room in one of the "safe houses" there. That evening his hostess, a French lady, asked him if he would like to listen to the B.B.C. He said, "Of course I would," and she took him to the house next door, where her neighbors, a sculptor, his wife and their son, were settled round the wireless set. The windows were all open, presumably because of the heat, so that anybody outside could have heard.

Introducing him to the circle, his hostess said, *"C'est un anglais; il vient d'arriver par parachute."* One of the group, being rather deaf, asked her what she had said, and she repeated in a very loud voice, "C'EST UN ANGLAIS; IL VIENT D'ARRIVER PAR PARACHUTE."

This was to be his temporary headquarters. It was, in fact, a meeting place of chiefs of the Resistance. Next door, at the sculptor's, instruction was given in the use of explosives. The explosives themselves were mostly hidden in the plaster casts.

He was living on the rations of his hosts, which were meager enough without having to be shared. Not feeling very happy about this, he mentioned that he had had to abandon a case of food in a haystack. This aroused everybody's interest, and they asked him where it was.

"Some five hundred kilometers from here."

"Do you think you could find it again?"

"Sure!"

So three of them set off, with empty haversacks, and took the train to Valence. In pitch darkness they made their way along the eighteen kilometers from Valence to the place where Starr had come down. He felt like a criminal returning to the scene of his crime, and was on tenterhooks lest somebody be waiting on the spot for him. He was able to go straight to the haystack, without any hesitation. The other two were very surprised that he should have been able to find it so quickly. But, although he had thought he had a good bump of locality, they were not so surprised as he was.

Now that they were here, he thought that they should make a proper job of disposing of the parachutes, so they pulled them up from under the earth that covered them and tramped with them to the Rhône. Starr wanted to throw the retrieved revolver in as well, but one of the boys pleaded so much that he did not have the heart to insist.

Then they went back to the case and opened it. To their astonishment, they found inside packets of Nestlé's milk chocolate, with English wrappers, and tinned foods such as salmon, all with labels printed in English. They packed everything into their haversacks and were able to make their way back to Antibes without incident. Starr learned later that food sent by way of boat to the French coast had English labels too.

At the sculptor's house sessions continued as usual. Starr noticed that there was a man who used to sit rather often on a seat not far from the house, apparently looking at the sea. Starr did not like it, and mentioned to the others that the man might be watching. They did not think so; but a day or two later a friendly gendarme warned them that a raid was going to take place. So they persuaded a would-be resistant to come along, in broad daylight, with his truck onto which they loaded all the dangerous stuff, and it was driven away to a safer place.

Shortly after this Starr was offered a small villa on the Cap de la Garoupe, where he stayed for some time and lived alone, which he found less nerve-racking.

His cover, which he thought out for himself, was that he was just a "Zazu." [1] His way of making himself unremarkable was to go about Antibes in a conspicuous pink shirt, with a bright yellow scarf, huge straw shoes and longish hair, carrying a box of paints and a canvas or

[1] A Bohemian artist.

two. He soon got to be a well-known and accepted figure, and as he passed a café someone would usually call out, *"Bonjour!"* As he could naturally talk in a genuine artists' jargon, the cover was complete.

It was from this spot that he used to leave occasionally on trips along the coast between Marseilles and Nice, carrying out his job of food expert — for he wanted very much to justify the title by practical work and was in fact able to do quite a lot. In Marseilles he managed to buy large stocks of dried bananas, wheat and chocolate, which were kept in wharves and renewed as fresh stocks came in. He organized a system by which any part of this stock could be delivered by truck, with good safe conduct furnished by the papers he obtained. He also became the proprietor of a flock of sheep. He did not have to look after these; he simply bought them and then they remained with the people whose concern they were.

He notified London of most of these moves, but received no reply. When it was approaching September 30, his daughter's birthday, he had radioed to his chiefs a request for them to buy a doll and send it to Michelle for the child — he had been told that commissions of this sort would be executed. Shortly afterwards a message came from London for him. It was simply: DOLL SENT.

About this time he became rather seriously ill. The food on which people on the Côte lived, whether in their homes or in the restaurants, tended to consist of four inevitable dishes, *tomates, tomates à l'aubergine, aubergines à la tomate* and *aubergines.* One night he woke up with horrible pains, unlike anything he had ever experienced. He dared not risk calling in any doctor except one belonging to the Resistance. Unfortunately, he had, on the next day but one, to meet someone in Marseilles, and despite his trouble he went. When he arrived at the "safe house" he almost collapsed, and his "contact" helped him into a bed in a storeroom at the back, then went out and after a while came back with a doctor. The doctor diagnosed *colique néphrétique,* and could promise no cure without a proper diet. It was quite useless his adding that butter and steaks would help more than anything.

As there was nothing else for it, Starr just had to carry on as best he could. His next task was to meet some people in Marseilles from whom he was to get some French money, in return for which a sterling account would be opened up for them in England. The francs had to be collected from Toulouse. Since to be found with so much money on his person would be fatal, he was accompanied — on the principle that a couple always appeared less suspicious than a man alone — by the well-known French singer Germaine Sablon, an admirable member of the Resistance, later decorated for her services. In the train on the way back they found themselves sitting opposite a man who recognized Germaine Sablon and revealed himself in his conversation as a pro-German Vichyite. He insisted on showing her a lot of diamonds that he was carrying, telling her how good business was now the Germans were in France, and how stupid the British were, and much more to the same tune. Starr got some jabs in his ankle from his escort's foot.

He began to feel by this time that he had gone as far as he ought to without further instructions from London, and none were arriving. He used to meet Peter Churchill occasionally, and discussed the situation with him. Churchill told Starr that as there was a felucca coming in a few days from Gibraltar, Starr might as well go back with it and ask in London for the instructions he wanted. And this they decided he should do.

It was now November. The boat was to come in to a spot near Cassis. Starr took various plans and papers, and was given several reports which Peter Churchill had collected. At Cassis he and some French people who were bound for England, including Claude Dauphin, the film actor, made their way to the place where the felucca was to come in.

It was a rocky, jagged coast, not unlike some parts of Cornwall, except for the mountains rising behind, and the night was very dark.

Shortly after signals had been exchanged they heard a slight lapping of the water, and then made out the shape of the rowboat which had been put down from the felucca coming towards them with several figures[1] in it. As the boat was made fast and the people climbed out, he held out his hand to one of them to give him a

[1] He was told later that one of them was "Odette."

pull — and found that the face he was drawing up towards him was his brother's.[1]

He knew that his brother was following in his footsteps in joining the French Section, but that was all he had known, and the meeting was totally unexpected. They stood talking for a few moments, and then, as his own party was settling in the boat, he had to join them. That was the only time that he ever met his brother in the field.

[1] Lieutenant Colonel George Starr, D.S.O., M.C., Croix de Guerre, Légion d'Honneur, code name "Hilaire."

III

Dijon

AFTER AN EXTREMELY rough crossing they arrived after ten days and nights in Gibraltar. Here Starr was given top priority, and, with his precious papers, was taken aboard an American Flying Fortress which was leaving for England. Back in London, he reported to Orchard Court, and was greeted with "Baa-aa-aa" on account of his flock of sheep.

For various reasons the S.O.E. was unable to send him back to France again immediately, and he was kept in England for several months. Michelle was still in Staffordshire, and he was able to be with her when their son was born.

While he was in London he saw Colonel Buckmaster, who was head of the French Section of S.O.E., several times, as well as Miss Vera Atkins, one of the senior officers of the section. He was also promoted to the rank of captain.

As he had been kept waiting around for so long, he asked to be sent up to Scotland to go through the toughening-up course again; before he had completed it, he was called suddenly back to London and briefed for his second mission.

He was told that this time he could drop some of the "security" — that, for instance, he need not spend so much time checking up and so on — as the "big day" would be coming off in two or three months' time.[1] He was, too, assured that whatever happened the men in the field could remember that they would be looked after. "If you are arrested, try to last out forty-eight hours," Colonel Buckmaster told him. Starr believes this was said to everyone, forty-eight hours being a reasonable time to assume it would take for the colleagues of an arrested man to get away from the area, after they had first removed any capital papers or other important things from any places where they had been working with him, or which were used or known by him. After this practically statutory period was up, the greatest danger to the captured man's colleagues was passed; providing his arrest had been known, he could reasonably expect that his comrades would have cleared out, and after this it did not matter so much if a little information did emerge in the interrogations.

Starr's new mission had nothing to do with food. He was to be organizer of a sabotage group. His code name on this mission was to be "Bob." He would be dropped during the April full moon, and this time was to be sent to the Departure School with a man whose Christian name was John, but whose surname Starr cannot remember. His code name was "Gabriel," and he was to be Starr's wireless operator. He said to Starr, "Buckmaster

[1] This, however, was only the spring of 1943.

told me, 'You will be in good hands, for Starr is completely reliable.' " One night they left for France, circled for about an hour over the Jura Mountains, where they were to be dropped, looking for signals, and twice got into position to jump. But both were false alerts and in the end, not having spotted the signal, they returned to England. The moon waned, and they had to wait a month before they could make a second attempt.

When the May moon had come they left again, but this time, just as they crossed the French coast, John, who was looking through the small window, said, "That must be France, but the blackout is bloody inadequate!" Actually, the plane was flying low over a Jerry mobile ack-ack battery, and he was looking down the wrong end of a searchlight, with the full glare of it in his face. The next moment shells burst around them, and one of the engines was hit and put out of action. The crew immediately jettisoned the containers they were carrying and everything else they could lay their hands on. The pilot managed to keep them airborne and returned to England, and after a very tricky landing got them safely to the ground.

After four more days they made another attempt, and this time, when they reached the Jura, the signals were spotted, and they jumped to a perfect reception. With them came a load of containers, and a reception committee was there with a truck in which to cart off the material. When everything had been cleared up they were taken to a house in a nearby village, where a pleasant room and very welcome beds were awaiting them.

Starr asked the man in charge of the reception committee how it was that a British lieutenant who should
have been there to meet him, and whom he knew, for
they had been on training together, was missing.

"We were expecting him," said the Frenchman, "and
don't know why he didn't turn up. Perhaps he's had
some trouble with his bicycle."

Starr was supposed to go with John to build up an
organization in the St. Etienne area. As the lieutenant
did not turn up either on the next day or the one after,
and there seemed no point in waiting for him any longer,
he decided to leave John in good hands and go first to
Clermont Ferrand, where he had to contact a certain
Guy, a wireless operator, and pass on to him a pretty
large sum of money and new codes which he had
brought from London.

When he arrived in Clermont Ferrand, he went to the
"safe house" where he was to meet Guy, and was told by
the people there that Guy had left the day before and
would not be back for five or six days. Starr waited
there, and during this time saw Maurice Southgate, alias
"Hector," whom he had known in France before the
war, and indeed since their childhood, who had come
like himself to the "safe house." Later he and Southgate
were to meet again, but this time when they were both
"guests" of the Germans.

In due course Guy arrived, and Starr passed over the
codes and money, had a good black-market lunch with

him and returned to Lons-le-Saunier, near where he had come down. As he left the station he saw one of the men who had been on the reception committee waiting outside — as he had been doing for several days, meeting every train that might bring Starr back from his mission. He gave Starr a slight sign with his head, then turned and walked away. Starr followed him through the town and joined him in a house on the outskirts. As soon as he had entered the Frenchman said, "We have learned that your lieutenant friend, who was to have met you on the night of your arrival, was arrested, either that day or the evening before, by the Gestapo. He is now in Dijon Prison."

This was terrible news. Apart from anything else, the captured man had been working in close co-operation with Guy, and Starr decided that he must take the next train back to Clermont Ferrand to warn him. Before going, he asked after John, and was told that they had got him fixed up and that he was being well looked after in a house with French Resistance people in St. Amour.

When he arrived back at Clermont Ferrand, he went to the "safe house," looked round to make sure nobody was waiting near the door, mounted the stairs, rang the bell and dashed down again, in case the place should be already occupied by the Gestapo. When the door above opened, he called out and asked the owner of the house, if it *was* he, to look over the banisters. The man did so, and Starr, recognizing him, called up, "Is everything all right up there? Can I come up?"

"Yes, it's all right. Come along."

He went up the stairs again and into the flat, knowing that his bad news was going to hurt them, as they were very fond of the lieutenant who had been arrested. To his surprise, he found the lady of the house and their daughter already in tears.

"What's the matter?" he asked. "Why are you crying? What's happened?"

They said that Guy had been arrested the day before. It was then that he had to tell them that Guy was not the only one, as the lieutenant had been arrested too.

He condoled with them, but said, "You must pull yourselves together. On top of all this bad news, I have some advice to give you which will not be very pleasing."

He urged them to leave the house immediately, sad though the idea might make them. He found that Guy had taken the codes, but not the money, and, after giving the French family something to carry on with, put the rest in his suitcase.

He then left, with the intention of getting out of Clermont Ferrand by the first train no matter where it might be going, and zigzagged through the town in a roundabout way lest he was being followed. When he got to the station he found a large crowd waiting before the ticket office, tried to get in front, but was sent back to wait in the queue. Just then a party of police made their way in, looked at the queue, came straight to Starr, and asked what he had got in his case. He had to open it, and of course it had too much money inside for an ordinary French citizen — thick wads of notes. So he just ran. As he thrust his way through the crowd the people, who were intelligent enough to realize what had happened, parted to let him through, but closed up again so that the police had difficulty in following.

He got out by one of the station doors, and then, instead of going on down the street, ran in again and hid among the freight, then dashed out and leaped onto the footboards of the train, which fortunately pulled out almost immediately. At the next station he got into a carriage. Then, at a further station, he changed and took the train back to Lons-le-Saunier.

There he saw John and had him transmit a message back to London to say what had happened, suggesting that he should stay on in the area and try to keep things going.

After this he met "Henri," a British lieutenant who had been working with Guy and the British officer who was now in Dijon Prison. "Henri" was the only real link he now had with the organization existing in the area, and through him Starr met several members of the French Resistance, and in particular "Martin," who was, "Henri" said, the best man he had.

It was through "Martin" that Starr was able to meet quite a number of French Resistance men — men whom he must necessarily know in order to carry on the job. He appeared to be an excellent worker, and Starr traveled very largely with him, meeting people wherever they went. "Martin" was always well received, and consequently so was Starr.

It was one of their big problems to find suitable places from which John could transmit, and wherever he went he had to be accompanied, as he spoke French quite fluently but with a grotesquely English accent. In fact, when they had met the reception committee on landing and John had spoken a few words, one of the Frenchmen had said, "*Eh bien, mon vieux, il n'y a pas se tromper. Il vaudrait mieux que tu parles le moins possible.*" Starr always thought it was very brave of John to come to France with such a disadvantage. He could not even go into a café on his own, and had to be very careful never at any time to speak too loudly.

They managed to fix him up in a medieval château up in the hills above St. Amour. After he had transmitted from here once or twice he left and went to a farm, and then Starr came to stay in the château.

He found this old castle a very weird place to be living in alone, especially at night. The atmosphere was most impressive, and he used to think of schoolboy stories, and to wonder if the people in the village down below would be saying the place was haunted if by any mishap his candlelight should be seen as he went from one room to another.

The caretaker supplied the meals, which he and his wife cooked in their little house outside the castle; and, although there was nobody living in the château, at midday he would go into the chapel and ring the bells, which became for Starr a signal for dinner. They would bring him in his meal and leave again, always locking the gates behind them.

Here he would occasionally meet "Henri," and later John came back from the farm so that they could work together, as they had messages to get away to London. Of course, in this rather depopulated area it was dangerous to transmit for any length of time from one spot, as they could have been rapidly located. As an extra precaution, John transmitted from the castle on batteries, so that if the Germans, in an attempt to locate their position, cut off the current section by section, the transmission would still carry on and no one would be the wiser.

A message had been sent under these extremely difficult conditions — a long way from London and in hilly country, which is bad for radio work — and Starr was very surprised and hurt for John when a message was received from their chiefs in London saying that his transmission was poor and that he should be more careful when sending and make some effort. John was a kind and stanch Englishman, very conscientious, and would never dream of doing anything but the best he possibly could. Starr felt he could not allow him to be rebuked in this way and, as his chief in the field, had him transmit back, in their next message, RECEPTION COMMITTEE AWAITING ARMCHAIR CRITIC. ICI ET LÀ ÇA FAIT DEUX. (In other words, "In the field one sees things differently.") Needless to say, this was not liked in London, and the reply they got finished with the words, END OF MESSAGE NOT APPRECIATED.

At about this time London sent out a girl to act as a courier for Starr. She arrived safely and was soon a very great help to the group. Her code name was "Pauline," and her real name Diana Rowden.

As time went on, with the help of "Martin" they managed to get together several sabotage groups, and Starr organized one or two sabotage jobs. In fact, they had the area pretty well covered. They had some difficulty in finding adequate fields for parachute operations, as nearly every time they found a good one London told them that it belonged to somebody else.

One thing he did which he really shouldn't have done. Having become the father of a son, he could not resist the temptation to go all the way to Normandy to tell Michelle's father and mother. Of course, when he reached the place where they lived, he disguised himself as best he could, since some of the people round about might recognize him. However, when he finally walked up the garden path and met his sister-in-law, she saw through his disguise immediately, took him by the arm and rushed him into the house, crying, "Papa! Maman!" Naturally they were extremely surprised and happy to see him, and overjoyed to have news of their daughter and grandchildren. He stayed just that one night.

On his way back through Paris, so that his trip should not be entirely useless to the section, he called on a couple of friends who had been fellow students of his, and arranged for his own flat to be used eventually as a "safe house" for any member of the organization who should happen to need one in Paris.

When he got to the Gare d'Austerlitz to buy a ticket back to Dijon, he was told that he would have to wait at least ten days even for standing room in the train. He could not, of course, stay away so long, and produced his special Vichy police card, signed by Darlan on behalf of Pétain — which had been obtained for him by a Frenchman, probably from someone who worked in the office where they were made out — and was granted a corner seat on the next train.

After meeting one or two important people in Dijon, he had to go on July 18 with "Martin" to Dôle. They had lunch together, and then set out in the little broken-down truck "Martin" used. As they came round a bend, after passing a big German-occupied aerodrome, shots were fired — not at them, but to bring up men — and in front of them they saw several cars placed across the road and a group of S.S. troops armed with automatic guns.

They had to draw up and were asked to produce their papers. The Germans went through their pockets and pocketbooks, and found on Starr the sum of thirty-five thousand francs. This was by no means an out-of-the-way sum for one man to be carrying, but the Germans declared that it was too much and that Starr and "Martin" must return to Dijon to have their identity investigated. They were handcuffed together, put between two S.S. men in the back of a car, and, with two other S.S. seated in front, driven to the local H.Q. of the "Gestapo," or, more correctly, the Sicherheits Dienst.[1]

Here they were unhandcuffed one from another and marched up the stairs. "Martin" was taken into a room on the second floor and Starr up another flight of stairs into one on the third floor. Here he had to produce his papers over again, and the German who had had him searched said that they would have to be checked.

Starr took out his cigarette case, which they had left him, and asked if the German would care for a smoke. This was not meant to be friendly, but had importance. The German declined the offer, but gave Starr permission to smoke, much to the latter's relief. He was then able to take the second cigarette from the right in his case and smoke the messages and the information he had prepared for London, which he always wrote in tiny letters on cigarette paper and rolled up with the tobacco.

After several more questions concerning his identity the German had him taken down to the second floor, with two S.S. to follow, and stopped by an office. Through the half-open door of the room he could see "Martin" standing in front of the desk as if he were undergoing the sort of interrogation Starr had just been through. The German officer who had interrogated Starr went into another room, slammed the door, and then, in a voice raised so loud that obviously he was intended to

[1] There has grown up a general custom of referring to the German Counterespionage Service, which had its H.Q. in France at 84 Avenue Foch, Paris, as the Gestapo. In fact, it was the Sicherheits Dienst (Security Service).

be heard, telephoned — or pretended to telephone — to the town in which "Martin" was supposed to live. He spoke as though he were checking "Martin's" identity with the authorities. Although he was speaking French, he pronounced the name "Martin" as in German. As soon as he had finished he came out of the room again and Starr was marched back upstairs. This all seemed to him very peculiar.

When they got back to the third floor the German said, "We have checked Martin's identity, and he is free to go. But we shall have to keep you in prison three or four days while we check up yours."

Showing as little reaction as possible, he said, "Why don't you phone Paris?" (the place where his papers were supposed to have been issued). Of course, he knew that this was hopeless, as no false papers, however well established, could stand up to a severe check. What really shattered him, even more than the prospect of imprisonment, was the appalling realization that "Martin," their "best man," was none other than a traitor working for the Gestapo. Otherwise, Starr reasoned, when the German had rung up to check "Martin's" papers, he would have found that they were phony. Starr's interrogator had obviously made him listen to the telephone call because it was to the German interest that he should believe "Martin" innocent; for if Starr subsequently escaped and went round telling everybody that "Martin" was a double agent he would become useless to them — hence the little theatrical act. His captors didn't seem to realize that their cunning defeated itself, for it was the very fact of the pretended telephone call, which they imagined must establish "Martin's" innocence, that proved to Starr his treachery.

"Oh, we can't phone Paris," replied the German. "It's too far away."

"Well, perhaps I could go to a hotel in Dijon and report here each day. There is no reason why you should put me in prison." Trying to look as unaffected as possible by all that he had just taken in, he was playing up to the German's game to make him believe he had swallowed the "Martin" story, pretending not to realize that he had been betrayed, and to be still thinking that he could bluff it out as an innocent man who did not understand why he should be locked up.

This show must have deceived the German that Starr still thought there was some chance of his being let out, for when they drove him to the prison, although they seated him in the back of the car between two S.S. as before, they did not handcuff him. On the way to the prison it was impossible to try to get out of the car, but as it passed through the archway of the prison into the yard and up to the door, he decided that the moment had come to make a dash for it. There was not much hope of escape, but as it was broad daylight and there were people about he thought that at least the incident might be seen, and in this way the news of his arrest might get back to the men he had been working with. This was very important, as it was the duty of anyone who had just been arrested to make the fact known if he possibly could, and thereby give his collaborators a chance to get away immediately. This was a protection for them in case he should crack under interrogation.

When the car came to a standstill the S.S. got out, and he stepped down calmly as though he were going to follow them, but as soon as he was out of the car he threw his trenchcoat in the faces of the men nearest to him and dashed to the archway. It was a good sixty yards. As soon as he started running, shots rang out, and as he was about halfway there he felt a twinge in his left side. He went on running, hardly aware of any physical sensation, managed to pass through the archway, and turned down a street to the right. Here for a few moments he was out of sight.

Not knowing the district, he turned right again, realized that he had entered a cul-de-sac, and had to turn back. By this time the S.S. had also come through the archway and were able to start shooting at him again as they followed him down the street. No car passed onto which he might have jumped, nor was there a bicycle anywhere against the curb. A bullet went through his left thigh. He staggered a bit, but managed to keep on running and turned up an alley to the right. But before he reached the end of it he found he could neither run nor even walk any farther.

The Germans turned into the alley and yelled at him to stop, which was quite unnecessary, as he had already done so. He could barely stand. They started walking gingerly up the alley. He will never forget the spectacle of three armed men approaching one who was obviously out of action and who stood only with an effort, their guns pointed at him, closing in on him very slowly, step by step, as though he might spring. They motioned him to get up against a wall. He did not move, and they came on even more carefully. At last they reached him, and, seeing that there was no possible fight left in him, grabbed him.

They took off his suspenders — presumably so that if he tried to run away his trousers would fall down — and, one still holding him on either side and the third brandishing his weapon behind, marched him back towards the prison. The people in the street had all stopped to watch and doors and windows were opening through which others gaped. This gave him some comfort, as it meant that the news would get around, and he felt that the diversion had not been in vain.

They took him into the prison and stripped him. By now he felt as if he were going to faint, but with a great effort of will managed to keep consciousness. They wrapped paper bandages round his wounds and he got back into his clothes. Then he was handcuffed, taken to a cell with double doors and locked in. The only furniture was a plank bed, on which he sat down, and a tin can in the corner. At the top of the wall opposite the door was a small barred window. Left alone, he felt the full force of his position.

Perhaps a couple of hours later the door opened and

two men came in, one in civilian clothes and the other in
S.S. uniform, with an S.S. rank about equivalent to a
corporal. This one, who was to be his interrogator while
he was at Dijon, began questioning him — where had
he come from, and so on?

Although he knew that they could get, if they had not
got it already, a good deal of his real story from "Martin," he thought it worth while to play for time. Con-
cealing the fact that he had recently come from England,
he maintained that he had been in France since before
the beginning of the war, somehow dodging internment, and had worked up a Resistance organization
in the locality, of which he kept all the threads in his
own hands, not telling too much to any of the people
who worked under his orders.

They listened to this story for perhaps two or three
days, allowing him to elaborate it in considerable detail, before telling him it was useless. To gain just a
little more time, he then told them the "cover story"
with which he had been provided in London.

This again they allowed him to tell at length before
saying, "They're all the same — the cover stories they
send you out with!" They then told him they knew the
organization he belonged to, and started asking direct
questions about the people he had met or been in
contact with, where he intended to meet his courier,
where his radio operator was transmitting from, and so
on.

He told them nothing at first, and then, as things

were getting pretty tough and he had more than accomplished his "forty-eight hours," with a good few to spare, he started to give them some information, but being very careful to give only that which "Martin" had. This he could do knowing that, since "Martin" was their agent, it must be in the possession of their service already. He gave it all very slowly, bit by bit, so as to make it last out, telling them of the places he had visited and the things he had done in the company of "Martin."

They let this go on for some time before beginning on questions to which they could not have had the answers through "Martin." To these he either replied that he did not know or gave them false answers. They became impatient, and from now on started punching his wounded thigh in an endeavor to help things along.

He said, "I've told you the truth up till now" (knowing that they could check it through "Martin"). "Why should you think that I wouldn't go on telling it?"

This did not go down, and the punishment continued.

For the first four or five days he had been interrogated in his cell, but from now on he was given a stick and had to get into the car with them every day and go down to the H.Q. of the Sicherheits Dienst in Dijon, where the questioning continued. There was considerable punching and kicking, and most of his body was soon black and blue.

There came an occasion when his interrogator was

called out of the room for a few minutes, leaving him alone in it. Starr noticed that he had left all his papers on the table, to which his own chair was quite near. Leaning forward, he was able to get his fingers on them, and turn them round so that he could read them. They gave him a great shock, as he found that they included a list of all the training schools of the French Section in England, and of the teaching staffs of each one. There seemed, as far as the establishments which he knew were concerned, to be no errors and no omissions. It was as complete as a school prospectus, and had the appearance not of something pieced together bit by bit, which would surely have contained gaps, but of something copied. This gave him a great deal to think about.

He turned the papers back again as they had been, and relapsed onto his chair before his interrogator returned.

Now the interrogator announced that he was going to go through the lists with Starr, who must provide a physical description of every member of the personnel. He read out the first name.

"About five feet nine inches, dark and thin," said Starr.

The interrogator wrote it down and went on to the next.

"Five feet five inches, medium height, ruddy complexion," said Starr.

He wrote it, and read the next.

"Five feet nine inches, thin and dark," said Starr. He went on to the next.

"Five feet five inches, ruddy complexion and medium stature," said Starr.

This went on for several hours, while Starr rang the changes on an astonishingly small number of details without arousing suspicion.

He noticed that the interrogator only went down the lists of the schools where Starr had been himself, passing any others. That again was interesting: they knew where he had been.

The afternoon passed and turned to evening, and they were still at this when it was getting late. At last Starr got tired of it.

"Five feet ten inches," he said. "That'll make it just a bit different, won't it?"

The interrogator started, looked more carefully at the many pages of particulars which he had by now written down, and realized the pattern they formed. This time he did not hit the prisoner, just sagged himself, and gave up for the night.

One day his interrogator showed him photographs of the lieutenant who had been arrested when he was parachuted into France, and of Guy.[1] He denied any knowledge of either. The wound in his thigh once more became a target. But he never recognized either of them.

Thanks to the treatment he was getting, his thigh now

[1] He learned afterwards that Guy was never brought to Dijon.

became so full of pus that his captors presumably
thought something must be done about it. Accordingly,
one morning the cell opened and a miltary doctor came
in, followed by five or six other men. As there seemed
to be no other reason for so many of them, he supposed
that they had come to enjoy the scene. They took off
his trousers, and the doctor approached with a long steel
instrument with a knob on the end, nominally designed
to draw off the pus. He pushed this right through Starr's
leg, in one side and out the other, from somewhere near
the knee on the inside, until the end came out somewhere near the buttock. Very conscious of the audience,
Starr managed to restrain the yell they were waiting
for, and to produce instead what must have been rather
a weird smile.

The commandant of the prison, an officer of the
Wehrmacht, had from the beginning stepped in to look
at Starr each morning, which he did as a rule with a
silent scowl. Starr was always just sitting there, with his
enormous fat leg stuck out in front of him, but never
without a smile on his face. It was on the morning
after this incident with the steel instrument that the
commandant, when he came round, clicked his heels and
gave him, instead of his usual glare, a military salute,
which he always did from then on.

Starr felt the solitary confinement very much. He had
fever and was mostly unable to sleep, as all night he
would be unable to stop going over and over in his
mind all the interrogations of the previous day, trying to

remember the answers he had given to each question, wondering if he had slipped up anywhere and said anything he shouldn't, and trying to foresee what questions would come next and to think what answers he should give. One night he was so tormented by thirst that he banged on the door and shouted for water, which of course was not brought.

During the first ten days he had very little other care, excepting the occasional change of bandages and a small amount of soup when it came round. He did not mind the lack of food at first, but after about ten days his appetite returned, and then he found that there was nothing to satisfy it with. All he got for the day was a small piece of bread, thrown at him each morning, which he would devour ravenously. Time and again he swore to himself that the next morning he would only eat a little of it, and would keep the rest of it until later in the day. But when the time came he always found that he could not prevent himself from eating it all immediately. In one way, however, this continual hunger was a godsend, because for twenty-four hours out of twenty-four his mind became incapable of imaging anything except mounds of chocolate — for some reason it was always chocolate — and so he was at any rate saved from going over and over the interrogations.

Trying to fix his attention on something concrete, so as not to become delirious, he would watch the sunshine moving slowly round his cell, and count the mosquitoes on the ceiling. The mosquitoes became very important because, as soon as night fell, they would "peel off" and dive in to the attack. He got quite expert in judging just how long he should let them bite before hitting them, and for one dead mosquito he would scratch a mark on the wall, trying each night to break the previous night's record. His highest score was forty-seven.

Although later, in the concentration camps in Germany, he was to suffer in a physical sense more seriously, it is still Dijon that he remembers most bitterly. He continually asked for a change of clothing, which he knew they had, since he had had a change with him when he had been arrested with "Martin," but they would not give it to him. He had to go on living in the same heavily bloodstained clothes, and his trousers were so stiff that they would have stood up by themselves. During the five weeks he was in Dijon he was never issued any paper for toilet purposes, and was never brought any water for washing. As he could never shave either, he must have looked the perfect jailbird when on one occasion they woke him up at three o'clock in the morning to take his photograph.

Every other day a Red Cross Wehrmacht man would come in to change his paper bandages, and although Starr could not understand German very well he could tell that this man was trying to say something encouraging. In fact, one day the German managed to convey to him that the Allies had landed in Sicily. *"Sie kommen! Sie kommen!"*

On the wall was a notice saying that when the door of the cell was opened the prisoner must stand at attention at the back of the cell and salute. Starr had never done this, and had no intention of doing so. But one morning, just to have something to say, he pointed to the notice, and asked the Red Cross man, "How should one salute? Like this?" — putting his hand to his forehead in the usual fashion — "or like this?" — putting out his arm in the Roman (Nazi) way.

The German peered around to make sure that nobody could see him through the half-open door, put out his arm in the Roman salute way, and said, *"So! Scheise!"* [1]

Starr concluded that he could not be a Nazi!

At the end of five weeks, his cell was opened at about three o'clock one morning, and he was brought water and allowed to wash and shave, and given the change of clothing he had so long asked for. Then he was handcuffed and driven to the Sicherheits Dienst H.Q. in Dijon. In the car, on the way, they told him that he was being transferred to Paris.

At the H.Q. of the Sicherheits Dienst he was kept waiting for some time in a room between two guards. The door leading into another room was half open, and through this he could hear a voice, which unhappily he knew very well, saying in agitated tones, "It's not for me. I don't mind about myself. It's for my mother. I'll do anything you ask me to do, I'd even sabotage any-

---

[1] A wholly untranslatable term of abuse.

thing in my home country, if only you would spare my life."

This seemed to be the answer to a number of the questions he had raised then, and in fact to many that might have arisen afterwards.

Shortly afterwards the man was brought out of the room and handcuffed to Starr, and they were taken out and driven to Fresnes Prison, on the outskirts of Paris.

IV
Avenue Foch

At fresnes he was taken to a cell, and this time was pleasantly surprised that there were already three other men in it. As soon as the door had closed behind him and they had shaken hands, he was assailed by questions, but this time they were friendly questions — though there were so many of them that it was practically another interrogation. He soon warmed up to his new companions, however, and began to tell his story. In fact, he was so glad to speak to someone that by the time he had finished telling them everything that had happened to him, and hearing all their stories in turn, they realized that they had been talking without interruption, except for eating, all that afternoon, all through the night and all through the following day. It was not until nightfall of the second day that, having temporarily exhausted themselves, they were able to think about settling down and trying to get a little sleep.

One of the prisoners was a Polish officer called Zbigniev, another Commert, a Parisian student, and the third Argence, a *garde forestier*. Argence had belonged to an organization connected with the French Section, and so far as Starr could make out it must have been with

the "Prosper" group, which covered Paris and the surrounding areas. Argence said that parachute drops had
been organized close to his home, and that a certain
amount of material had been cached somewhere near.
When the Germans came to arrest him they asked him
to show them where the stuff was hidden. He would
not tell them, but they quickly pointed out that it was
useless to deny anything or to refuse to take them to
the spot where the material had been buried, and produced an accurate map on which was shown the exact
spot. Later, when he was brought to Paris, he was shown
copies of all the written communications which had
passed by plane between the "Prosper" group in London.
He thought it astonishing that the Germans should be
so well informed; obviously they knew pretty well everything that was going on between London and the men
in the field. A very great many other people had been
arrested at about the same time as himself.

After they had finished exchanging all this information, conversation calmed down and finally dwindled
out. For Starr this place, where he had friends with
him, was like heaven after Dijon. Nevertheless, the others
said, "Now that we've finished telling our stories we
shall start mooching around again and time will drag
on as it did before you came."

Starr said, "Oh no, it won't! We've got to do something about it."

"What can we do?"

"In the first place, from now on, every evening after

lights out we shall go to the cinema. Each one in turn
will relate as completely as possible a film that he remembers well." In the daytime, he suggested, they should
take their socks off and roll them up into balls, and they
managed to have quite exciting games of bowls,
much to the amusement of the guards, whom they could
see peering in occasionally through the peephole.

When the novelty of this wore off he taught them
"twenty questions," and they also played "prefixes" and
even such childish games as "I spy" — though there was
not much to spy in the cell.

One day they chanced to notice that there were still
some grains in the straw of their mattresses. They took
some of these out carefully and decided to try to grow
them. Commert had a little pot which had once contained food, and when they were taken out one day for
exercise in the yard they each managed to scoop up some
grit and bring it back and put it in the pot. They planted
the grains, watered them carefully, and every day put
the pot in the sun, moving it round the cell so as to keep
it always in the patch of sunlight. To their huge delight,
shoots came up, which they tended lovingly. But one
day an S.S. man came round inspecting cells, and demanded to know what their "garden" was, and threw it
out. They had become so attached to it that they nearly
cried.

After this they filled the cracks between the floor
boards with grit, and planted some more grains in that.

When about three weeks had passed, somebody at last

came to fetch Starr from his cell. His companions, realizing where he was going, sang out to him to pinch a few fag ends from the ash trays and bring them back.

Then he was taken in the "Black Maria" to the H.Q. of the Sicherheits Dienst in Paris, at 84 Avenue Foch.

Here he was taken up to the top (fifth) floor and left, with the other people who had come in the "Black Maria," to wait in the guardroom. After a little while he was taken into the next room, and met for the first time the man who was to be his chief interrogator here, and whom he afterwards always heard called Ernest.[1]

The atmosphere at this interrogation was quite different from that at Dijon. There was no rough stuff, and it was all quite civilized. Nevertheless, although Starr had to undure no physical pressure or discomfort, he found this interview quite as great a strain as anything that had gone before, since he realized that he was now in the hands of a man with a brain. Ernest believed nothing at all of what Starr had told his questioners at Dijon.[2]

[1] Ernest was half Swiss. He had lived for many years before the war in Paris, and was not a member either of the S.S. or of the Nazi Party. He was attached to the Sicherheits Dienst in 1940 as a civil auxiliary, in the first place as a translator and interpreter, but was by this time himself interrogating the major agents of the French Section.

[2] When I met Ernest in 1950, to ask him if he could give me some information about "Madeleine," whose story I was then writing, he told me something about Starr's interrogations at Dijon. He said that Starr had told their men there a story that was as good as a novel, which it must have taken days to write down, making out that he was the chief of an independent resistance organization, of which he kept all the reins in his own hands, trusting his assistants with very little information. Ernest said, "It was a very brave thing to do. He made

At lunchtime Ernest had his lunch brought in, and ate it off the corner of the desk. A plate came in for Starr too — they had the same — and the interrogation went on during the meal.

Sometime during the daylight hours, S.S. Stürmbann-führer Kieffer, the head of the Sicherheits Dienst in France, came in, and for a while conducted part of the questioning. He was a thickish-set, fairly bluff sort of man.

After he had gone out again Ernest carried on the questioning until quite late at night, Starr being very careful not to add anything to the information they had. Ernest showed him copies — probably the same that Argence had seen — of a great amount of correspondence which had passed by Lysander between the agents in France and London.

During the evening Ernest took him back into the

---

it appear that he was the only one it would be worth trying to get anything out of, and this impressed me very much. He told it with so much conviction and so many elaborate and supplementary details that he even made our men believe it for some days. I admired his inventiveness as well as his courage." When he studied Starr's file, which had been sent up with him from Dijon, Ernest realized that it recorded nothing but fictions, for Starr had always spun a new story as soon as the one before had broken down, and during his five weeks' interrogation there the staff had gained from him no information at all.

Ernest also said, quite spontaneously, "Starr was badly treated in Dijon. He had a bullet wound in his thigh and they hit him there during the questioning until it swelled very much."

Ernest said further that when he took Starr in hand he fared no better than his predecessors, and although he devoted much time to questioning him, never learned anything either. "Starr was one of the rare agents of the French Section whose arrest had no distressing consequences for his collaborators," he told me.

guardroom to meet another British officer. It seemed strange to Starr to see this officer sitting by the wireless, quite comfortably, listening to the music and reading a book. Ernest asked Starr if he knew this man, and asked the other if he knew Starr. Fortunately, they had never seen each other before, and so were able to deny recognition quite truthfully. He learned later that this was "Archambault," the radio operator attached to "Prosper's" group, which covered the Paris area. He had been kept at the Avenue Foch since he had been captured at the end of June, the time when the big roundup had taken place of which Argence had spoken to Starr in Fresnes Prison.

When it got really late, he was given something to sleep on in the guardroom. It seemed to him that he had hardly gone to sleep when it was morning and Ernest was waiting for him, ready to start again immediately.

The interrogation went on during the whole of this day. In the evening Kieffer came up again with a map of France, which he laid before Starr. On this map were marked off twelve areas, representing districts covered by members of the French Section who had been arrested, and covering in all about three quarters of the map of France. The districts were numbered from 1 to 12, and each contained the code name or names of the agents who had been arrested. Kieffer spoke to Ernest, and Ernest said, "The chief wants you to fill in your area."

After he had done so, Ernest said, "Write in the number thirteen and your code name, Bob."

He did this, printing BOB in capitals.

Kieffer suddenly looked delighted, but Starr could not think what his source of pleasure could be until Ernest explained, "He likes the way you print. How do you come to be able to draw letters so well?"

"I'm a poster artist in civil life. That involves lettering."

There was some more conversation between Ernest and Kieffer, and then Ernest said, "He wants to know if you will copy out the whole map again, printing all the names in the same style, as it's so messy."

Starr said he would think about it, and Ernest told him that he could give them his answer in a few days, when he would be brought to Paris again for further questioning.

At about ten-thirty that evening he got back to his cell and his comrades, with the precious fag ends he had collected from Ernest's ash tray.

He told them what he had seen and learned and of the request that had been made to him. It had occurred to him that if he did undertake this copying he might, when it was finished, be given more to do. He might even become permanently installed at the Avenue Foch, where he would be bound to gather a great deal of information from all the papers presented to him, and from where, also (since it was only a converted private house), it ought to be easier to escape than from Fresnes.

His three companions listened with interest and en-
thusiasm, and agreed that it would be worth trying to do
this and to carry the information back to London.

About three days later he was fetched from his cell
again. "If I don't come back in a few days," he told
them, "you'll know the plan has started to work."

He told Kieffer that he would do the copying, and
when he had finished — having in the process learned
the map by heart — what he had hoped for actually
happened, and he was given another to do. After that he
was presented with slips of paper with "family trees"
showing the organization of all the networks of which
the Germans had knowledge, not only those operated
by British agents belonging to the French Section, but
also those owing their allegiance to General de Gaulle.
Naturally, he learned an enormous amount.

To do this work he used to be brought out of his cell
on the top floor of number 84 — one of the seven re-
served for prisoners considered to be, for one reason or
another, specially interesting, whom it was desired to
keep on the premises — and installed at a table in the
guardroom. This was next door to Ernest's room, and
a vantage point from which he could see and hear much
of the life of the place, and gather what was going on.

He was glad to be able to have some words with "Archambault" again soon after his return. Having had
a talk with him, he realized that there was nothing
wrong with the man at all, as he had thought on his
earlier visit, when "Archambault" had been so com-

fortably seated in the guardroom. He strolled around the place looking very much at home, but it did not signify anything that should not have been.

From "Archambault" he learned that not only had the Germans been able to make copies of the messages in transit between France and London; they were also operating the radio sets of some of the captured wireless operators. London was continuing to make deliveries in response to the messages sent, but of course straight into the hands of the Sicherheits Dienst. "Archambault," indeed, told him that he had revealed his own code, but had not felt overworried about it because he had not given his "security check," without which any message purporting to come from him should not be accepted in London as bona fide. His interrogator at the Avenue Foch — presumably either the radio specialist, Dr. Goetz, or else Otto, the head of the radio department — had then said, "Yes; but you haven't given me your security check." As he put it in the singular, "Archambault" guessed that although they knew there was a "security check," they did not know there were two parts to it, so he gave him the first check, keeping the second to himself. Goetz then had a message transmitted to London without the double "security check," which in "Archambault's" mind was as good as having said to his chiefs, "This is not your man who is transmitting to you." He was flabbergasted when, on being taken down to be interrogated after the reply had come from London, he was shown the return message, which contained the words, "You have forgotten your double security check. Be more careful." [1]

"Archambault" was kept for quite a while in the Avenue Foch before being eventually sent elsewhere, and Starr was able to talk with him several times — though never alone.

He learned more about the mass of arrests that had taken place at the end of June and the beginning of July, and that "Prosper," the overall chief of all the sectors in the Paris area, had given to Ernest and Kieffer the names and addresses of all his collaborators, on a formal

---

[1] "Archambault" probably counted not only on the absence of the proper security check, but on the difference in the operator's tap, to warn London.

A former agent of S.O.E. who served in the field as a wireless operator told me she and those who trained with her were told at the wireless school where they were sent in England that every operator's tap on the machine was individual, like handwriting, and that if they were captured it would be "impossible" for another person to take over in their stead without the difference being detected by the operator receiving in England. To make doubly sure, recordings of their performances were made before they were sent to France, so that should London at any time become uneasy as to whether the tap was still the same they could check with the record. If all the operators sent out were given this confidence in the ability of London to detect a German attempt at imitation, this is a fact which should be borne in mind when judging those who gave away their codes.

I spoke to Ernest about this matter, and he said that nobody had been more surprised than they were at the Avenue Foch when London accepted the false messages. He, of course, did not work in the radio department, but he understood that an operator's work was always followed carefully by their service from the moment they became aware of it, and perhaps recordings were made. At any rate, the substitutions were always made by a man who had listened in to the operator while he or she was still at large and who had imitated the performance when he took over. They had taken pains over these forgeries; even so, they were surprised at their success.

promise that their lives would be spared. (See A NOTE ON
THE "PROSPER" GROUP, page 66.)

Starr was also told by Ernest that Kieffer had obtained
from Berlin the authority to have the lives of captured
agents of the French Section spared; and it was understood that they would be kept in custody until the end of
the war, when, no matter who won it, they would presumably be freed. Ernest regarded this as a very special
grace which Kieffer had obtained for these prisoners.[1]

As time went on Starr saw many other prisoners who
were brought in, only a few of whose names he can
still remember, and, even so, at what dates and in what
order he is uncertain.

Some time that autumn he saw Peter Churchill and
"Odette" briefly, when they were brought up, probably
for the day, from Fresnes, where they were kept. At one
moment he was fetched into Ernest's room, where
Churchill was standing with Ernest and Kieffer, and
they asked him whether it was true that Peter Churchill was the nephew of Winston Churchill. As this
must obviously have arisen from something Peter had
said, he replied, "Certainly."

Later either Ernest or Kieffer, or both of them, came
into the guardroom and told him that Peter Churchill
and his courier, "Odette," maintained that they were
married, and asked him if this was true also. Again he

[1] Ernest still believes that this authorization was really obtained by
Kieffer from Berlin, and that faith was only broken in Germany
during the latter phase of the war.

felt that he must support the story, so he said, "Of course. They're a very well-known couple in English society."

One day Ernest came to fetch Starr, saying, "I've got a friend of yours here. He's heard your voice and he would like to see you."

He was taken into Ernest's room and found himself facing Rabinovitch, whom he had known from the beginning. They greeted each other, and exchanged a few words, but could hardly say anything very interesting with Ernest presiding. Starr was anxious for Rabinovitch, in case, being a Jew, he should get treated worse than the others. Later Kieffer, who came into the guardroom after having seen the new prisoner, remarked, "He's a Russian Jew!" However, he did not say this as though it had any fateful significance; and in fact Starr did not think that Rabinovitch received any ill-treatment while at the Avenue Foch.

Later the two of them spoke a little further — though again they were not alone — when Rabinovitch was brought into the guardroom to choose a book from the shelves. Rabinovitch, alias "Arnaud," with whom Starr had worked for a while during his first mission in the South of France, had told him earlier that he had only just managed to escape when Peter Churchill and Odette were arrested. After this he had gone back at once through Spain to England, and had been parachuted a second time. This time the radio set through which the landing point was arranged was one of those operated by Kieffer's men, and so he was met by the Sicherheits Dienst. He was very sore about all this.

One evening, when Starr was sitting at his table in the guardroom, Ernest brought in a man whom he had been interrogating. Starr recognized him — he had seen him at the Departure School in England when they were both about to leave on their separate missions — and, without thinking, he said, "Hullo!"

The man recoiled with the words, "I don't know you!"

He had been met on the field by the Sicherheits Dienst, having been dropped from England in response to radio messages sent by one of the captured sets, and brought straight to the Avenue Foch. In a flash, Starr realized that what the Germans would not know was that this was the new prisoner's *second* mission, and that he had retorted "I don't know you!" because he was afraid Starr might reveal that the last occasion on which they had met was just before he had been parachuted over to France some months ago — and if the Germans knew that there had been an earlier mission they would question him about it.

Ernest had, of course, taken in the little scene, but he did not say anything for the moment. He took the man into a cell, then came back and asked, "You appeared to recognize that man. Do you know him? Who is he?"

"No; I don't know him really," Starr replied. "I must have made a mistake. It's got something to do with his mustache."

Fortunately, Ernest did not press him any further, but left it at that.

Starr worried a certain amount about this slip. A day or two later, however, the man was brought into the guardroom to select a book and took the opportunity of saying to him, "I'm sorry I said I didn't know you the other night. If I'd known then what I do now, I'd have said I *did* know you, because then you could have helped me as you do the others."

Starr felt much relieved that the other realized he could be relied upon not to give anything away. By "help" was doubtless meant the cigarettes Starr was able to give prisoners who were brought in.

Of course, his position could give a false impression, just as "Archambault" had at first given *him* uneasiness. And it could lead to unfortunate incidents, as on the occasion when a prisoner who was brought into the guardroom after interrogation, seeing Starr at his table, thought he was another official. He came up to him and said, "I'll do anything you want. Absolutely anything. *Really*, I will!"

"I'm British," said Starr.

The man — in Starr's words — "was not French."

When Starr had caught up for the time being on the copying of "family trees," Kieffer said that he would like a portrait. Starr replied that in order to make a good job of it he must have proper materials, and so Ernest took him, with two S.S. men, back to Starr's home in

Issy-les-Moulineaux in order that he might fetch them. When they got out of the car, Starr noticed that Ernest and the two S.S. stood a little back, so that he went up to the door alone. The concierge, overwhelmed at seeing him, flung his arms round his neck, crying, *"Cher Monsieur Starr!"*

Starr said, "Take care. I've got the Gestapo behind me."

Ernest, who had both seen and heard, came up, and told him that he should not have warned the concierge in this way. From Ernest's point of view, the chance of some interesting conversation had been lost. Starr decided to count on the fact that Ernest was human, and spoke to him in the sincerest way. He said, "You must understand that you are occupying this country by force, and that there is a sense of oppression. A Frenchman doesn't have to belong to the Resistance to be glad to see an Englishman." [1]

While Starr was collecting his drawing materials, Ernest found a wireless (an ordinary receiving set) which he said he must take along with them, and the S.S.

[1] Ernest told me this story from his own point of view when I met him. He had stood back, and a little to one side, as Starr went up to the door, so that the person who opened it should not see him. Then he had just seen two arms come out and encircle Starr's neck. No face was visible. Starr had said, "Gestapo behind me!" and the arms had shot back as if they had been stung. He had come up to Starr and scolded him for saying that, because it had spoiled any possible value from his point of view, and they had had a moment's argument. He supposed that the concierge must have gone back into his room, but he walked with Starr straight past to the lift and did not distress him by peering in.

began invading the kitchen and carrying out saucepans
and frying pans and other cooking utensils. Starr protested, "The wireless is fair game. But my wife is coming back here to live in a few months, when the Allies
have returned to France, and she will need her frying
pans and her saucepans. I want them put back."

Ernest told the S.S. to take the pots and pans back
into the kitchen and put them where they had found
them. And so they returned with the drawing materials and the wireless.

Kieffer could not spare much time for sitting for his
portrait, and he gave Starr a photograph to work from,
coming up from time to time to see how it was getting
on and to make comments. He was, in a way, quite
friendly. On Sunday mornings he would come round to
each of the prisoners' cells in turn, open the door and
give biscuits, chocolate and cigarettes to the inmates,
exchanging a few words. The food was, in any case, excellent, since the prisoners had the same as the Germans.

One night Starr heard that the Sicherheits Dienst had
arranged with London for a parachute operation which
was to take place on a field comparatively near the Paris
area. Kieffer had never been with his men to receive a
parachute delivery, as most of the parachutings so far
had been some way away. Now that there was going to
be one so near he thought he would like to go too and
see the fun. A big party went off down the stairs together, Kieffer looking as excited as anything, and taking
his Sten gun with him. The next morning Starr learned

that they had had a disappointment, as, through somebody's mistake, they had gone to wait on the wrong field.

That morning Starr drew a couple of cartoons. In the first they were all going down the stairs, looking very formidable, Kieffer in such haste that he was pushing his men right and left, and one was falling over the banisters. Under this he wrote the title, DER SPRUCH IST DURCH! (THE MESSAGE IS THROUGH!) In the second picture they were on the field. All except Kieffer had given up and were lying on the ground, having covered themselves with hayricks, just their feet and heads sticking out. Kieffer alone had not abandoned hope and still stood, stalwart, searching the sky above him with his long-range torch. In its beam he had caught a bird, flying over with a large grin on its face and R.A.F. markings under its wings, from which a large drop was descending, evidently destined for his head. The title of this one was: DER ABWURF (THE DROP).

Starr left both, inadvertently, on the table in the guardroom.

Some nights later, he was waked up in the small hours by Kieffer, who opened his cell and put the light on. "Did you do these?" he demanded blusteringly.

Starr blinked at them, and said, "Yes."

"*Prima! Prima!*" exclaimed Kieffer, laughing. "First-class!"

Starr learned the next morning that the S.S. had had a big dinner at a Paris hotel, and that, someone having

pinched these cartoons from among Starr's papers, they
had been pinned up on the wall where Kieffer would see
them when he came in to take his place at the head of
the table.

⟨∾∿∾⟩

A NOTE ON THE "PROSPER" GROUP

As the "Prosper" affair has been considerably discussed
in France, it may be of interest to quote what Ernest
writes about it:

Nearly all the letters sent by "Prosper" and "Archambault" to the head office of the French Section in London
were intercepted by our Service and a photostat made, after
which they were forwarded. Through these letters (containing detailed accounts of the activity of the "Prosper"
Sector and the parachuting grounds, together with the
B.B.C. messages indicating the parachutings due) we learned
the addresses of "Prosper," "Archambault," "Denise" (their
courier) and their principal [French] collaborators and their
letter boxes. This allowed us to arrest nearly all the members
of their organization at one stroke. When "Prosper" realized
the extent of the disaster, and when he saw the photostated
copies of the reports he had sent to London, as well as of the
radio messages sent by "Archambault" and the other wireless
operators, which had been deciphered by our specialists in
Paris and Berlin, he decided to tell the whole truth, on the
formal promise of Kieffer that neither he nor his collaborators should be either killed or ill-treated.

I think it is wrong to consider "Prosper" as a traitor. To
understand him, it is necessary to realize the situation in

which he found himself. He saw himself betrayed, and wished to save his men from being shot or ill-treated. I knew "Prosper"; and he was a loyal and very good Englishman.

To appreciate the importance of Ernest's statement, it should be understood that the "Prosper" Sector, covering the capital, had considerable ramifications. "Prosper" was not only organizer of the British team in the Paris area, but overall chief of a whole plexus of French Resistance networks attached more or less closely. Colonel Buckmaster, in his book *Specially Employed*, writes that "Between Beauvais and Tours, and between Chartres and Melun, he had formed dozens of small groups, totalling perhaps 10,000 men and women . . . who welcomed his assistance and relied on his radio link with London."

Madame Balachowsky, wife of Professor Balachowsky of the Institut Pasteur, gave me some information which would seem to tie up with Ernest's statement. The professor was the head of a French group working under "Prosper," which had its headquarters in a small place called Grignon, to the northwest of Versailles, where "Prosper" himself and the rest of the British team, "Archambault," "Madeleine" and "Denise," also had their working headquarters. She told me that in the fortnight following the arrest in Paris, on June 26, of "Prosper," "Archambault" and "Denise," roughly fifteen hundred French people in surrounding and even faraway districts had been arrested. (These included her husband — who later returned from Buchenwald — and be-

tween twenty-five and thirty people personally known
to the Balachowskys in Paris itself.) Hoping to achieve
something for her colleagues, she sought an interview
with an official at the Avenue Foch shortly after the arrests had been made, and he referred to the coup as
"*notre plus belle oeuvre*" — "our finest job yet" — in
France.

After the war she came to England and presented
the evidence she had collected concerning this disaster
to the chiefs of the French Section. They did not attempt to dispute it, and looked glum. They said they
did not know how it had come about.

To prevent too much blame from being laid to the
door of "Prosper" — of whom the Balachowskys speak
with great regard — it should be borne in mind what Ernest says, that before he had been captured all the most
important information had been given away in the intercepted letters. This written matter, greatly supple-
menting the radio messages, which were necessarily
short and couched in the language of telegrams, would
have been sent, as was the practice, by such occasional
planes as came down to the ground — for instance, to
pick up somebody whom it was desired to bring to England. But how this mail came to pass through German
hands at the Avenue Foch is a mystery still unsolved.
Not even Ernest knows. Probably the only person who
could have told was Kieffer. It was, in any case, left
to "Prosper" only to give secondary information;
the Germans had the main layout of his organiza-

tion, with its key places and the addresses of his key people, before they began on their series of mass arrests. He gave further people into Kieffer's keeping, but honestly believing that it was for their protection, since if they were to be arrested without his co-operation (as he had little reason to doubt they would be, sooner or later) he would not be in a position to stipulate for their good treatment, which he could do as the price of facilitating Kieffer's work. In a ghastly situation, knowing the ground to be gone from under them all, he had decided to use his own discretion and judgment. It was the irony of the situation that in a later phase of the war, when these people passed out of Kieffer's hands — possibly into those of officials who did not appreciate the solemn promise which had been given in respect to these particular prisoners — they (and he) were all killed.

The Balachowskys told me that "Prosper" had begun to feel before his arrest that their operations were perhaps all the time known to the Germans. After his return from a short visit to England early in June — just a few days before the blow fell — he had been most overcast, and spoke to them of his doubt whether they were not being betrayed from a quarter that he could not locate. He said he had even hesitated to return to France, but felt that he must rejoin those for whom he had become responsible.

2

During the second week of October 1943, a prisoner was brought in who was to become involved in Starr's story. This was a young girl, "Madeleine," [1] a wireless operator.

Starr saw her for the first time as she was being taken to the bathroom one morning, and after that they would say "Hullo" to each other when she was brought into the guardroom to change her library book. It was not possible to have conversation. He learned from Ernest and others that she refused to give information, and he had great regard for her.

However, one night he heard "Madeleine" crying — her cell was opposite his — and in the morning he felt he must get some word of comfort to her. It had occurred to him that it should be possible to exchange messages by means of written communications, which

[1] Noor Inayat Khan, G.C., M.B.E., Croix de Guerre with Gold Star. She was half Indian, spiritual and cultured. She had been landed in France on June 16, 1943, to work in the Paris area. Originally destined to serve as assistant to "Archambault," she had carried on after the great disaster in which he and "Prosper" were arrested. Declining an offer from England to fetch her back, she had continued working, very much on her own, throughout the summer, linking herself up with such French groups as she could find and connecting them with London, until on October 13 she was captured.

In her room were found her radio set and a complete file of back messages. These, when they had been deciphered, yielded her code. Ernest does not think she ever knew that her set was afterwards operated by the Germans. At any rate, he never told her. It would have been a needless cruelty, for it served no interest of his service that she should know.

The discovery that she had been arrested was made in London in April 1944.

could be concealed in the lavatory in a crevice formed where the wall met the undersurface of a small basin. The problem was how to get the first communication to "Madeleine," telling her to look in this place.

At his table in the guardroom he wrote a message which began, "Cheer up, you are not alone, perhaps we shall find a way to get out of here," and went on to describe the crevice in which he thought they could leave notes for each other. Then he told the guard that he wanted to go to the lavatory, and took with him not only the note but a pencil. As the door of the lavatory was visible from the guardroom, the guard never bothered to follow him up to it. Just before he got to the lavatory door he let the pencil drop, as if by accident, stooped as though trying to pick it up, caught it with his foot and sent it rolling further on; then he made another apparent attempt to get hold of it and caught it with his foot once more, this time sending it round the corner into the passage where the cells were. As "Madeleine's" cell was only just round this corner and he was already in a stooping position, it was the work of an instant to push the note under her door.

On his very next visit to the lavatory he found an answer from her, thanking him and telling him that she was in communication through the wall (they tapped in Morse code) with a French Colonel Faye,[1] who had the next cell to hers.

[1] Léon Faye, Colonel Breveté de l'Armée de l'Air, military chief of a French Resistance organization, *L'Alliance*, captured on September 16, 1943.

Now the three of them began to consider possible means of making a triple escape. The cells were curiously constructed rooms, very high for their breadth and length, with no windows in the walls, but with a square aperture in the middle of the ceiling, across which bars had been placed. Above this again was a sort of square funnel, leading up to a window that opened on a rod at the top. This window could obviously be opened if one could get up to it; the problem was how to remove the bars across the aperture in the ceiling.

One day the young woman who used to clean the floors, Rose-Marie, looked in at the guardroom to say that the carpet sweeper had stopped working. None of the guards offered to help, but Starr jumped up and said that he understood carpet sweepers. They allowed her to bring it in and give it to him, and he turned it upside down and began to take it to bits knowledgeably. The Germans became restive as the dust got up their noses, and asked how long it was going to take. He said it would be quicker if he had tools, and they told Rose-Marie to fetch him her toolbox. In it there was a screwdriver, which he would dearly have loved to keep, but dared not, as the guards were too interested.

Starr's work on the carpet sweeper did not last very long — he had not intended that it should. In a few days Rose-Marie came back to ask if she could give it to him to put right again. This time he managed to retain the screwdriver; but as he thought it would be dangerous to take it to his cell immediately he found a temporary hiding place for it. Since there was central heating in the Avenue Foch, the fireplaces were not in use, and were covered by metal screens with a door which could be opened to reveal the grate. Working on the floor in the neighborhood, he chose his moment, opened the door a little, pushed the screwdriver in and closed it again. If Rose-Marie should report the loss of her screwdriver, and it should subsequently be found in this place, he could plausibly deny responsibility. Why on earth should he have wanted to put one of Rose-Marie's tools in the grate?

A few days passed and no one mentioned the affair, so he retrieved the screwdriver and left it for "Madeleine" and Faye, stuck by the point into the crevice under the basin in the lavatory. He thought they could use it to mine the plaster into which the bars were set. It would be sufficient if they could bring out even one bar. His own problem was how to get up to the frame in the ceiling. Since to move his bed from one side of the cell to the middle, under the opening, would arouse suspicion, he moved it, in the first instance, simply from one side of the cell to the other.

The guard, when he came in, expressed astonishment and went to fetch Ernest, who asked him why he had moved the bed.

"To look at the room from the other side," replied Starr. "Just to make a little change of view."

As there was no furniture in it except the bed, this might have sounded silly, but Ernest did not see anything suspicious in it, and said it was all right.

A few days after this Starr moved it again and put it against the wall opposite the door, then across a corner, and by the time it came to rest in the middle, under the opening, the guard had lost all interest in its movements.

Starr was not, however, very tall, and found that, even now he had got the bed into the right position, he would still need something to climb on in order to reach the bars and draw himself up through them. Accordingly, he took a chair from the guardroom. The guard, seeing this, frowned and fetched Ernest.

"I have nothing to hang my clothes on," Starr explained. "I just have to drape them over the end of the bed at night, and it isn't doing them any good. I thought you wouldn't mind my having one chair out of the guardroom."

"That's all right," said Ernest, and let him keep it.

Starr could get up to the bars now, and he discovered that, unlike those in "Madeleine's" and Faye's cells, they were fixed with ordinary screws into a wooden frame attached to the ceiling. These screws would be easy to take out. There was still one thing that worried him about the actual escape. The switches controlling the lights in the cells were in the passage. Consequently, as prisoners liked to read at night, the guard on duty had instructions to come round occasionally and knock on each of the doors and ask the inmate whether he wanted the light out yet. He naturally expected a reply. Starr thought that he could stay up late and engage the guard in con-

versation while "Madeleine" and Faye were climbing
out; but after that he would have to get out himself. It
might take him some time, and it would be most awk-
ward if the guard came on his round just then. Starr
could not fail to reply, and if he was somewhere near the
ceiling his voice would betray his position.

One day he saw a bit of electric cord with a switch on
it lying on the floor in a corner of the guardroom; so he
took it into his cell. The guard came in while he was
fiddling with it, and seemed to think it irregular. Once
again he went and fetched Ernest.

"I'd like to be able to put my light on and off myself,"
he said. "Then I can be independent of the guard. He
won't need to come round to me any more."

Ernest thought that was a good idea.

One day an S.S. man left his cosh on a chair in the
guardroom; so Starr took this, too, and hid it in the fire-
place when the guards' backs were turned. He was not
really sure of the practical utility of this trophy and consulted Faye. Faye said he would like to have it; so, after a
day or two had passed and the S.S. man did not seem to
miss his cosh, or at any rate to have reported its loss,
Starr redeemed it and left it in the lavatory.

During this time he had continually the pain of seeing
other men brought in, in response to the messages sent
over the captured radio sets. The Germans would tell
him, "We're going to meet another of your boys tonight!" It was torture to be told about it, to be unable to
prevent it, and later to see the doomed man brought in.

By the November moon an agent called "Antoine" [1] was parachuted to a field arranged by the Poste-"Madeleine," duly met by the Germans, and brought back to Paris.

In November, also, while the preparations for escape were going on, John, alias "Gabriel," Starr's former wireless operator, and "Pauline," his courier, were brought to the Avenue Foch. The Germans said to John, as they brought him up to Starr, "Here's your old chief!" "Pauline" he saw only briefly.

John was put into Starr's cell on the first night. This very unusual proceeding seemed to him most significant and sinister. Two men who had been working together would not be put into the same cell for shortage of space. He felt that the situation was very dangerous, and John realized it, too. The temptation to talk was enormous; yet, knowing that someone might have crept up to listen at the door, or that there might be a concealed microphone, and that in any case John would be interrogated the next day, and perhaps Starr also would be questioned anew, they hardly dared to say a word.

---

[1] A South African major. He had worked in the field with "Madeleine" during the early summer, returned to London by the August moon, and then been dropped again by the November moon to the field, where he was met by the Sicherheits Dienst. Ernest, who interrogated him, said that he spoke in great anger of those in London who had sent him, and seemed to think that they had sacrificed him deliberately, for he called them "murderers." In general, Ernest found that the men who had been met on the field in this way were very bitter against London. "Madeleine" was not allowed to catch sight of "Antoine," and Ernest felt sure that she did not learn that he had returned and was a prisoner. He was later executed in Germany.

John did, however, tell Starr how he had been arrested, which obviously the Germans knew already. Another man had been sent out from London to work with him; but the radio through which the arrangements were made was one of those worked by the Sicherheits Dienst, and his intended colleague was met on the field. Within twenty-four hours he was escorted by the Germans to his rendezvous with John, and even greeted the latter with a personal letter which he had brought out from England.

John had received a cruel grilling at the local H.Q. He had not brought his radio set to the rendezvous, and they had tried to make him reveal where he had left it. He showed Starr his backside, which was all the colors of the rainbow, and said that he had been made to bend over and had been beaten with a belt. He had suffered so much that he had been afraid that if they began again the next day he would break down and tell them where his radio set was.

After their night in the cell together, John was, of course, taken for interrogation by the Avenue Foch staff. During the course of the morning, also, Starr was taken down the stairs to the office of Otto, the head of the radio department. John was not in the room. Otto greeted Starr with, "Well, were you pleased to see your friend?"

"Not in this place."

"I expect you had a good talk."

"No. It wasn't interesting for us."

"What? Didn't you want to know what he'd done

with the radio set? It's your responsibility, as his chief."

"I didn't ask him, and he didn't tell me. Do you really believe that we should be foolish enough to fall for a trap like that?"

John was, of course, questioned intensively, as his radio set was something which Kieffer's men wanted. Naturally, they wished to operate the Dijon area, where he had been working, as they were doing others. Nevertheless, he was not hurt at the Avenue Foch. He never revealed where the set was, and, Starr is sure, never gave them any information at all. The Poste-"Gabriel" never worked for the Germans.

After the first night John was put into the cell next to Starr's, and when a few nights had passed, and Starr felt that they were no longer under such surveillance, he tapped through the wall to John, in Morse, telling him that an escape was being planned and that he could have a screwdriver with which to get out his own bars, if he wanted to come too. John replied, however, that he had given his word of honor not to escape.[1]

Faye and "Madeleine" had been passing the screwdriver backwards and forwards between them; Faye was the first to get his bar free. Then the screwdriver came back to Starr. It was short work to take his screws out,

[1] Ernest told me that it was he who suggested to Kieffer that some of the prisoners of the French Section might be asked for their parole. Kieffer said, "But we should have them climbing out all over the place!" Ernest said, "No; not Englishmen—not if they have given their word." Kieffer agreed to try the experiment of allowing parole to one or two. In fact, Ernest said, none of those who gave him (Ernest) their word attempted to break it.

and he passed the screwdriver back to "Madeleine" to finish off her job. She was to tell them when she was ready.

The remaining problem was that of ropes. These were indispensable as, when they got out, they would be on the top of a five-story building and have to find a way down. Having no sheets, they would have to make ropes from their blankets, in spite of the tendency of blanket material to tear. As they did not know the layout of the roofs, or the length of the drops for which they would have to calculate, they decided to carry their blankets intact and to tear and knot strips as they were needed.

While taking all possible measures to secure the success of their plan, Starr thought it prudent also to provide for the event of its failure. Having caught up, for the time being, with the copying of the slips concerning individual agents and teams, he had been given a prodigious document to do in which this matter was set out in full with all its interrelations. He took his time over this, making the beauty of the work an excuse for its slowness. Kieffer was enjoying watching it grow, and Starr thought that if they were recaptured his desire to see it finished might deter him from having Starr shot.

While their preparations were in the final stage, Ernest was wounded by an agent outside, and so was no longer on the scene.[1]

At last "Madeleine" signified that she was ready, and

---

[1] He received seven bullets in the body on November 19 from a British agent named "Hercule," and spent some weeks in the hospital.

it was decided to go at midnight. It was November 25.

Starr now wrote Kieffer a letter, which he hoped would help them if the escape did not succeed.

As you will have realized when you get this, we are trying to escape. Now that I hope we shall not be meeting again, I should like to thank you for the good treatment we have received here, and to say that we shall not forget it.

Wishing you the best of luck in the chase that will follow, but much better luck to ourselves.

BOB

Kieffer, he thought, would find the sporting touch irresistible.

Then he put together the notes he had written out on tissue paper for London, with all the information he had gathered about the German control of the radio sets.

He sat up late that night, working on Kieffer's portrait, and at the appointed hour, when the other two were supposed to be removing their bars and climbing out, tried to engage the guard's attention while slowly getting together his affairs with the utmost clumsiness and noise. Even so, tell-tale sounds from the cells were clearly audible to him, but not, apparently, to the guards, who were not listening for them.

When all was quiet, he said he was going to bed, and a guard followed him to his cell and locked him in.

He put the chair on top of the bed, climbed up and removed the loose bar, and struggled up between the other two, on which he was then able to stand in order to reach the window. Faye was at the top, waiting to give him a hand out.

"Where's 'Madeleine'?" he asked when he had got out beside Faye.

"I don't know. She hasn't come up."

Together they picked their way across the roof to the window above what they calculated must be "Madeleine's" cell, and peered down. To their great disappointment, they found her still imprisoned, working feverishly round one end of the bar, which was still firmly set in the wall. Perhaps she had not liked to take it right out in order to test whether it was free for fear of not being able to get it back again.

They opened the window and took turns leaning down and working with the screwdriver themselves. This must have gone on for two hours at least, or even three. The noise of the screwdriver grating against the iron was sickeningly loud, and they were afraid every minute that it would attract somebody. At last the bar came away and Faye pulled her out and kissed her.

They knew that certainly one of the adjoining buildings in the Avenue Foch was occupied by the Sicherheits Dienst, and feared that the other might also be. They decided, therefore, that they should make their way along the roofs of a line of houses that flanked, on one side, the courtyard at the back of number 84, and on the other, a street running at right angles to the Avenue Foch. These houses had, unfortunately, slanting roofs, French type, over the top of which it was impossible to climb, and they were on the side which looked over the courtyard.

On the far side of the courtyard, opposite the back of 84, they could see, however, some houses with flat roofs, and thought that from these it should be possible to get down into the street. To gain these they had to walk the length of the side of the courtyard along a ledge only two or three feet wide which ran beneath the gutter. Five stories up from the ground, and carrying blankets, it was not a pleasant walk. The ledge even had a slight tilt towards the courtyard. Faye went first, "Madeleine" next, and Starr brought up the rear.

Near the end they came to a raised circular structure, onto which they had to climb before they could get down the other side. To get up onto it with the blankets, without slipping, was not easy. On the other side they found a drop down to the flat roofs which would necessitate a first use of their "ropes." They tore some strips of blanket — not too thick, as they would need more for whatever further descents lay ahead of them — knotted them, tied one end to a vertical that they found and slid down. Now that they had got so far, Faye was almost irrepressibly jubilant. "We've done it! We're away!"

At this moment an air-raid siren sounded and their hearts sank, because whenever there was a raid the guard came round the cells and their absence must be discovered. They began hurrying across the flat roofs, but at this moment found that they were being swept by long-range torches from the fourth floor of number 84.

They fell flat on their faces, hoping not to show up against the skyline. Then the torches were extinguished and they jumped up again and ran on.

They had to go up a little iron staircase and then found themselves looking down onto the street, now only four stories below. A window below them, they saw, had some sort of projecting ledge in front of it, and they decided that they must get down onto this. While Faye and "Madeleine" were making further ropes, Starr went down the iron staircase again, and buried his precious notes in some flower pots which he had noticed. If they were to be recaptured, as now seemed almost a certainty, to have these found on him would make things much worse.

He rejoined his companions. Faye now abandoned the cosh, which he could not carry while climbing down such a rope. He went first, broke the window with his elbow, and climbed into the house. "Madeleine" followed him, and Starr brought up the rear as before. Now that they were inside, they found themselves in pitch darkness, and began to make their way down a long and winding service staircase. Almost to their surprise, no lights were switched on, and nobody came out of any of the rooms to ask them what they were doing. They reached the ground floor at last, made their way to the front door and opened it.

Here their hopes fell finally when they found that they were in a cul-de-sac, an enormous brick wall having been built right across the road. They could see men with torches passing and repassing the open end of the road, and realized that the S.S. had put a cordon round the block. They were pretty well bound to be recaptured now, whatever they did, but Faye thought they might as well make a fight for it and try to break through the cordon, so they began creeping along the road, as close as possible to the side, their shoes still about their necks as they had had them from the start.

When they got to the corner Faye made a sudden spurt forward. There was an immediate spluttering of automatics, and he was seized and taken away.

"Madeleine" looked round at Starr as though to say, "What do we do now?"

He touched her arm and made a motion with his head indicating that they should go back.

They turned round now a little aimlessly, found the door of the house they had come through still open, and went up the front staircase this time, to the second floor, where they found a door opening into what appeared to be a sitting room. Still in the dark, they groped their way in among the furniture and sat down on what seemed to be a couch, side by side. He thinks they began to talk in whispers, though he cannot remember what about.

Suddenly a woman's voice rang out, "Who are you? What are you doing? Are you thieves?"

Looking round, they could make out the head of a woman peering at them over the banisters.

Just then the front door opened below, lights were

switched on and S.S. came swarming up the stairs. They were seized and marched out.

Back at 84 everything was in commotion. Kieffer walked over to them in a towering rage, and said, "You're all three going to be shot." On the landing of the fourth floor they were stood together with Faye, in a row for execution. Faye said, "I have only done my duty!" One of the S.S. struck him in the mouth.

The automatics were raised, but before giving the order to fire Kieffer waited while they were searched. In one of Starr's pockets a guard found the photograph of Kieffer from which he had been doing the portrait and handed it to his chief.

Kieffer asked, "Why were you taking my photograph with you?"

"A little souvenir," said Starr.

A very faint smile began to go up one side of Kieffer's face; then it straightened again.

Starr said, "I left a letter for you. You'll find it in my cell."

Kieffer sent one of the guards up to look for it, and they waited until he came down. All this waiting and conversation was making it much more difficult for Kieffer to have them shot in cold blood.

The guard came back with the letter. Kieffer read it, and it was fairly obvious that it had reached something in him. At the same time he glowered again. He stood now looking at the three faces lined up in front of him against the wall, from one to the other and back again.

Starr watched the movement of every line of his face. It was obvious that a terrible battle was going on inside him. At length, instead of giving the guards the order to fire, he just said that they should be taken upstairs and that he would come and see them later.

V

Word of Honor

THE THREE PRISONERS were now separated. Starr was put back in his cell with his wrists and ankles handcuffed, and left on the floor, from where he could look up at the tantalizingly open window. The handcuffs were so tight that it was impossible to get to his feet, and he could move about the floor only by wriggling.

The next morning the cell was opened by one of the guards who had been searching the roof, and who was holding in his hand the cosh which Faye had had to abandon. Leering down at Starr, he exclaimed, "So you were going to hit us with this, were you?" and began to belabor him with it. Luckily for Starr, this was stopped when somebody came by and saw what was happening.

Later he was transferred to what had been Faye's cell — he did not know what had been done with Faye — where the bar had been replaced. Here he was left, still handcuffed.

During the whole of the next fortnight nobody except his guards came to see him, and the handcuffs were never taken off his hands or feet for any purpose. The guards would bring him meals and put them within his reach, and he would sit up as best he could, and, with a bit of maneuvering, would manage to carry the food to his mouth. At times he would bang on the door, and the guards would come, take him by the back and lift him to his feet, and half help, half carry him to the lavatory, where everything was accomplished with great difficulty.

After a fortnight of this he was freed and taken down, very stiff, to see Kieffer in his office on the floor below. Kieffer asked him if he would finish copying out the big document (to which he agreed), and if he would give his word of honor not to make any further attempts at escape.

Starr had got himself transferred from Fresnes to the Avenue Foch with the intention of collecting information, escaping with it and taking it to London. All that he had since learned made it even more imperative that London should be informed of the situation — namely, that it was the Germans who were now transmitting to London on some of the captured radio sets, and that the British were in consequence continually sending out men to be met on the field by the Sicherheits Dienst. He found himself, therefore, placed on the horns of a dilemma. If he refused his word and was sent to Germany to a concentration camp or a prison, one thing was certain — that he would never, from such a place, be able to convey any message to England. If he remained at the Avenue Foch, however, it was possible that he might find some way of getting the information out without himself escaping — for instance, by passing it to another prisoner who had not given his parole, or even to someone working there. He said, slowly, "So long as you keep me *here*, I give you my word of honor that I shall not attempt to escape. If I should be sent anywhere else, that promise will be no longer binding."

Kieffer accepted the reservation, adding that, if Starr broke his word, twelve other members of the French Section would be shot.

Starr was now reinstalled at the table in the guardroom. "Madeleine" and Faye had disappeared from the scene, and he was not told what had become of them.[1]

Shortly after this a change was made in the use of the rooms on the top floor. Since Ernest was still in the hospital, the room which had been his office became the guardroom, while what had been the guardroom — it was very small — became Starr's daytime workroom. He still did his work at the same table, but was now alone, and therefore less in contact than before with what was going on. On the other hand, as he had given his parole he was allowed to have the door open, and so he could see people pass. The guards, from Ernest's former room next door, could also keep an eye on him, but he had no longer the

[1] "Madeleine" and Faye had been asked for their word of honor, by Kieffer, on the morning of their recapture. Both had refused to give it. In consequence, they were sent to Germany on the same day, November 26, 1943, traveling together as far as Baden, where they were separated. On the twenty-seventh they arrived at their destinations, "Madeleine" in Pforzheim, Faye in Bruchsal. Both were ordered to be kept in chains, though in "Madeleine's" case the prison staff had them removed after a time. Later both were executed, "Madeleine" on September 12, 1944, in Dachau, and Faye on January 3, 1945, in Sonnenburg.

possibility of exchanging a few words with a prisoner brought in to wait with the guards.

Apart from "Archambault" and "Madeleine," he never had spoken contact with any of the radio operators whose sets were being worked back to London.

In spite of his parole, the only places between which he could go unescorted were his "workroom," his cell, the lavatory and the bathroom. If he had to go down the stairs, he was always accompanied by a guard who walked behind holding a pistol.

He thinks it was not long after he had been put on parole that Kieffer came to see him, looking very overcast, to tell him of a terrible thing that had happened. The Sicherheits Dienst had a house on the Place des Etats Unis where they kept some of the prisoners belonging to the French Section. In one cell were two men whom Kieffer had asked to give their word of honor that they would not escape, telling them, as he had told Starr, that if either of them subsequently broke faith, twelve other members of the French Section would be shot. They had, as Kieffer learned afterwards, already begun breaking a hole in the wall at the back of a cupboard at the time when he asked this question. One of them had refused to give his word and had been handcuffed; the other had given it, continued tunneling and escaped.

Kieffer said that he would have to do as he had threatened, and find the men to be shot. He told Starr, "It may be that you must be one of them."

"*Tant pis*," replied Starr.

This, however, was the last he heard of it. He believes that some men were shot, though he does not know if the full number was made up.

One evening a party of Germans, including one called Placke, came in together talking about a restaurant in which they had been having dinner.

Starr said, half jokingly, "Why don't you take me out to dinner?"

They took it up and said, in the same half sportive way, "Why *don't* we take Starr out to dinner?"

They asked Kieffer and, almost to their surprise and certainly to Starr's, got the reply, "So long as not less than five of you go with him, and you never leave him."

Thus began a real game that was to be played from both sides with different intentions.

On the evening arranged, they all went downstairs together. Now that it had come to it, Placke was a shade nervous, for, as they went down, he said, "I know you've given your parole to the Stürmbannführer [Kieffer], but I should be glad if you would give it again, for tonight, to me personally." Starr replied that he had given it, and once was enough.

They drove to a smart restaurant, where they found a table for six, ordered everything that was good on the menu, and finished up with cigars.

After this began a series of incidents, though Starr cannot be quite sure of the exact order in which they happened.

This Placke had substituted himself for an officer of

the French Section who had landed in the north of France with the object of being organizer of an area round St. Quentin, but who had been met on the field by the Germans, for the rendezvous had been arranged with London by one of the radios operated by the Sicherheits Dienst. A message was sent to say that the man had arrived safely, and from then on Placke ran this sector of the French Section himself, building up the network with genuine Resistance men and linking it up with others. He did not look too German, and spoke English well enough to deceive any Frenchman who tried, out of politeness, to address him in his "own" language.

Obviously it paid the Germans better to let such a network build up, under their control, until it reached a certain size, rather than arrest immediately the first handful of patriots with whom they found themselves in contact. And, on the French side, the fact that weapons really were dropped from the skies, as Placke had promised, seemed to be an assurance that the organizer was a man from London.[1]

One day a British plane was brought down in Placke's

[1] Ernest told me that, as a secondary consequence of this situation, French people several times brought to Placke British airmen who had crashed, and whom they had been hiding in their houses, asking him to have them sent back to England. They supposed that he could arrange for an R.A.F. plane to come down to the ground to fetch them. This was a development he had not foreseen, and he did not immediately know what to do. The fugitives were made prisoners, of course, but as they were members of the regular forces, not secret agents, were not prisoners that the Sicherheits Dienst would normally hold. In the end, he believes, they were sent to ordinary prisoner of war camps, not concentration camps.

area, and Starr was asked if he would go with Placke and see if he could identify the bodies. It was highly unlikely that he would be able to, and if by chance he did recognize one of them he could deny it, so he agreed. They went down and got into the car, with two S.S. guards, and drove off. On the way Placke stopped somewhere to collect a woman.

Some distance outside Paris they stopped in front of a building, and Placke went in with the woman. He did not reappear until it was too late to keep the appointment, so they had to come back without having done anything.

On their return, Placke told some cock-and-bull story to Kieffer. The two S.S. said nothing, and Starr, who had in fact never left the car, did not spill the beans either. It was not the only time that Placke lied to his chief.

On another occasion Starr was asked if he would go with a party of the Sicherheits Dienst to a field where there was to be a parachute operation. He decided that there could be no possible use to the Sicherheits Dienst in his simply standing there on the field, and he might as well have a sniff of fresh air. If he gave the impression of being a little bit amenable he might gradually gain a greater liberty of action, which he must do if he was to devise some means of getting information back to London. At the same time he realized that, as his simply accompanying them on this expedition could have no concrete utility, they must have asked him to go with them in order to create a psychological atmosphere, and that

they were trying to work him up to the point where he
would do something real for them. As it happened, on
this occasion something must have gone wrong, because,
although they waited most of the night, no plane came.

One day he was told that London had asked them to
find a field for a plane — a Hudson, if he remembers
rightly. They did not know how much space a plane of
this type would require, and took him with them to help
find a suitable field.

A party set out, including, he remembers, Goetz, of the
radio department. The Germans found quite early a
beautiful field, which he had to find some means of dis-
suading them from using. At first he could think of nothing to say against it, and could only suggest by a grimace
that it left something to be desired. Then, as luck would
have it, he spied a party of German soldiers coming up
the road and hoped there might be a barracks near.

"This is no good at all!" he said.

"Why not?"

"Too many *Boches!*"

Goetz was annoyed and said, "That's enough of your
cheek!" It was the word *Boche* that had riled him. But
they drove on.

After that they looked at a lot of fields, and Starr managed to pooh-pooh them all. The light was going, and it
was no longer easy to see the ground in the dusk. The
Germans were getting steadily more tired and crusty.

Finally, Starr made them stop the car beside an enormous field. He got out and walked to the gate, then a lit-

tle way into the field, with one of them. The ground
was very rough and changed levels so often that no plane
could easily have landed on it. Also there were two or
three agricultural instruments right in the middle, and
he had noticed a German listening post across the road
at the other side of the field. Knowing that the R.A.F.
always photographed a field that had been chosen for
them before sending a plane to come down on it, and
that they would certainly reject this one when they saw
the photograph — on which the listening post would
show up — he declared, "This is your field!"

The German, deceived doubtless by its size, accepted
his decision, and when they got back to the car one of
them marked the place on a map they had brought.

Not only would no R.A.F. plane come to that field,
but Starr hoped that the people in London would wonder why one of their men should have given them such
an impossible location, and smell a rat. He thought that
it should not be beyond their powers of reasoning to
work out that that field must have been chosen by a
prisoner in his circumstances. If they got this far, then
they must realize that one, at least, of the radio posts was
German-operated.

During maneuvers of this kind he often wondered if
he would make any kind of slip. It was, of course, much
more dangerous than just sitting in his cell, in the sense
that once outside all sorts of contingencies might arise
that he had not been able to foresee, and he might, unless he were able to think very clearly at all times, put a

foot wrong. At the same time, it was these unforeseeable contingencies that gave him the best chance of doing something or making something happen which ought to perplex London, and cause them to realize that all was not well with their networks in France.

It was not an easy road to have chosen: it was full of possible pitfalls, and demanded that he should be always alert to a complex situation and to all the different implications that any action of his might have. On the other hand, supposing that he did make some kind of slip, and the Germans gained some small profit out of an action of his, it would, he thought, be such a drop in the ocean, considering all that was going on around, that the game would still be worth the candle, for the sake of the possibility of informing London of the real situation.

One day Kieffer brought up a shabby-looking wireless, complaining that he had asked London, by one of the posts they controlled, to send a really first-class wireless set, and in reply this miserable thing had been parachuted from a Mosquito. He put it down in front of Starr and asked, "What d'you think they mean by it?"

Starr knew at once what it was, and that London had really sent them what they asked for. He had seen sets like this in England when he had been shown over an "art of camouflage" section. It was one of the very latest type, camouflaged in the frame of an obsolete model.

He pretended to be puzzled for a moment, then burst out laughing.

"What are you laughing at?"

"English sense of humor! Don't you see? They must have realized at last that it's you who are transmitting to them. If it had been you, I suppose you would have dropped a bomb on the reception committee. That would have been your Jerry idea of a joke. Our boys have dropped you this little bit of nonsense — just to let you know they know!"

Kieffer was not sure whether to be satisfied with this answer. He had a message transmitted back to London, repeating that he had asked for a first-class set of the latest model, and asking what they meant by sending this thing. A reply was duly received, saying that what they had sent *was* the latest model, and explaining how to discover the real works under the camouflage frame. Kieffer told Starr, chuckling.

On another occasion he was taken out in the car with Placke and some others to point out to them the kind of places that members of the French Section would choose as objects to sabotage. He presumed that the reason Placke wanted this guidance was that London had been pressing him to undertake some sabotage in this area, and he wanted, without blowing up anything of real importance, to have something he could tell them that he had done.

Starr pointed out one or two objects of minor importance — bridges, railway lines, and so on — as suitable targets. When they got back he made out a report for Placke on the day's activities, but as he alone had taken notes it was child's play to deceive them. He referred to hilly country where it was flat, wooded country where it was bare, and indicated the roads and railway lines and targets in the wrong places. If Placke tried to find them again, in order to blow them up, he would have difficulty; and if he contented himself simply with sending to London a list of the targets supposedly destroyed as "jobs done," then the people in London, if they looked for them on the detailed maps they must have, should realize that there was something wrong.

Eventually the Germans asked him to do something serious. Placke had received a message from London saying that they were sending a plane over his area with a man in it who would talk with him (their organizer, as they thought) by S. phone.[1] The very fact they proposed holding a conversation in this way, without sending their man down to the ground, suggested that London had at last become uneasy about this sector, and Starr hoped that his attempts to sabotage Placke's work were beginning to bear fruit. Placke's English was not good enough to deceive an Englishman, and if he tried to do the talking himself the whole show would be given away. So the Germans asked Starr if he would speak through the S. phone to the man in the plane. He replied that he would think about it. This was about a fortnight before the conversation was to be held.

The matter needed very careful consideration. He considered the possibility that if he took the S. phone he

---

[1] A device enabling someone on the ground to hold a conversation with somebody in an airplane in flight.

might, as he would be speaking to the man from London direct, be able to inform him of the situation. But the Germans understood English, and would stop him as soon as they realized what he was doing. He tried to think of some very short phrase which would contain all the necessary meaning, but decided that anything adequate would contain more words than he could possibly get out before a hand was clapped over his mouth. The man in the plane would perhaps think only that the S. phone was not working. He would have to think up something else.

During the days that followed they asked him several times if he was going to do it, and each time he replied, "I'm thinking about it." Evidently they were confident of being able to bring him to the point, for they did not make any other arrangements, as he was afraid they might do if he refused point-blank.

The great night came, and just as they were about to take him with them he said, "I've thought about it. I won't do it."

They were exasperated. They had one man on the staff who spoke English better than any of those present, but they had sent him away on a mission. It was decided that Von Kapri, who belonged to the radio department, would have to do it.

"You can take the earphones and listen," they said to Starr. "You can do that, can't you? You can tell us if you recognize the man's voice."

He thought there could be no harm in this — it might

be interesting to listen to what went on. If by any chance he did recognize the man's voice, he could deny it.

The party set off, waited on the field, and at length a droning was heard and the plane approached. Von Kapri took the S. phone and Starr earphones. The man in the plane began speaking. Von Kapri said a few words, his German accent noticeable despite all his efforts. The man from London did not speak again and the plane went away.

Starr felt much better after this, as he felt that it should be the end of Placke's little game in the north.

2

After the fiasco with the S. phone the Germans did not badger him again to go out with them; probably they understood now that he had only been leading them up the garden path.

The game with the radio sets still went on. Apart from the Englishmen who lost their lives in consequence, very many Frenchmen went to their deaths. The Resistance organization which had been allowed to form around Placke was a dreadful instance: when at last it was decided to arrest the patriots, they were all shot.

Either on Christmas Eve or, more probably, New Year's Eve, Kieffer came up a few minutes before midnight with a tray on which were bottles of whisky and gin and three glasses. He fetched John from his cell and poured out glasses for all three of them, raised his own glass and said, "Good health!" and they drank together. After that he left Starr and John to pour themselves some more drinks and to talk as late as they liked. However, they were careful what they said!

During November and December, Starr, who had finished the big map some time ago and had since been kept occupied with other work of the same kind, was busy drawing first Christmas cards and then New Year's cards for the Stürmbannführer and other members of the staff to send to their families and friends. But besides these he had also done one for Kieffer on his own account, and had taken great care with it. He gave it to him when he came up some time during the morning of January 1.

On the outside was printed simply: 1944. Kieffer opened it, and a Tommy in battle dress jumped out, pointing a rifle with fixed bayonet at him.

This time he did not laugh. He looked at Starr, his face serious and almost anxious. "Do you really think so?" he asked.

Starr said he was sure of it.

Kieffer did not argue, and it was plain that it had cast a gloom on him.

In January, Ernest came back, but Starr did not see so much of him now, since, his old room having become the guardroom, he was given an office on a lower floor.

Starr had not had his hair cut since his capture the previous July, and by this time it was halfway down his neck. So one day Kieffer had a barber come in to cut it.

By an extraordinary coincidence it was the same barber whom he had always been to in civil life. The man started when he saw Starr, and as he was cutting his hair whispered, "I could get a message out for you."

This offer was too quick to be genuine, and Starr did not trust his expression, so he replied, a trifle coolly, "No thanks. It wouldn't be worth it." [1]

He thought sometimes about Buckmaster's promise not to abandon them at any time, and would stand at the window looking down into the broad avenue, with its gardens beneath. Sometimes he would fancy that one of the figures sitting on a seat was looking up as though he were watching the place, and would try to show himself at the window and make signs — though the Germans stopped him if they caught him doing this. He never got any evidence of response from below.

He had the wireless on most of the time in his room, as the guards did in theirs next door, and could always turn the knobs himself, although it was forbidden to listen to any but German-controlled stations. One day he had been listening for some while without any of the officials being about. When they came up he looked at them anxiously and said, "Are you going to take us down to the cellars with you?"

"What? What are you talking about?"

"Well, I know it's forbidden to listen to stations that aren't German-controlled, but I've just had on the B.B.C.

[1] He went to look for the barber's shop after the war, and found that the man had disappeared.

news in French and it says they're going to bomb the Avenue Foch." [1]

Nobody doubted that he had really heard this or troubled to check it. They had never before stopped working on account of alerts, but from now on a new regime was instituted. Every time an alert was sounded they all went downstairs and did not come up again until after the All Clear. But they left the prisoners locked in the cells!

He did in fact get the B.B.C. sometimes when there were no officials about; the guards did not interfere, and he was occasionally able to impress them by giving them news of an event before it was published by the Germans. At first they jeered and said he was making things up, but afterwards, when they found that they got the confirmation later in the German announcements, they became interested to get the news in advance. Some of the guards were Russians, or, more exactly, Georgians, who had been conscripted into the S.S., and they were thrilled when he was able to get the news in Russian for them. They would not have dared to tune in to a forbidden station themselves, but if he liked to do so it was his crime, not theirs, and they would come in from next door to listen. Once he had gained their confidence he could do a little propaganda, interpreting the bare announcement of events in a light always strongly favorable to the Allies.

[1] The B.B.C. did sometimes announce beforehand their intended targets in their transmissions to France, so as to give the French workers and people living near a chance to get away.

In fact, some of the officials, too, realized that he got the B.B.C. Even Ernest would sometimes look round the door and ask, "What's the news, Bob?"

On one occasion, as he was turning the knob, he got an orchestra playing *God Save the King*. He could not resist the temptation to turn up the volume control as far as it would go, and the national anthem resounded deafeningly in the Avenue Foch. Kieffer burst in, shouting, "Stop that church music!" (The Germans have a hymn to the same tune.)

Winter gave way to spring, and Hitler's birthday was observed by the staff with due gravity. When Starr was taken down to Goetz's room, for some reason that he cannot remember, he found them all seated round a table, in full uniform, wearing their decorations, with stiff collars right up to their chins, holding themselves very erect and looking in fact rather uncomfortable.

This struck him as so funny that he could not resist straightening up himself also, and gave, for the first and last time in his life, the Nazi salute, but with the words, "*Heil* Churchill!"

This brought a laugh. Placke was especially amused. The next time he came up to the guardroom he gave Starr the salute, with a big smile on his face, also to the words "*Heil* Churchill!" In fact it tickled his fancy so much that he did it on a number of occasions after this.

Starr never saw or heard of anything in the nature of torture while he was in the Avenue Foch, but the fear of it was often very strong in prisoners who had just been brought in. Sometimes they had had bad experiences in the provincial H.Qs. where they underwent their first interrogations, and this had led them to expect still worse things when they came up to the Avenue Foch. One day a Frenchman, Pierre Brossolette, an agent of one of the networks owing allegiance to General de Gaulle, was brought into the guardroom. He was told to sit down, which he did for a moment, then got up and walked to the window. The guards did not realize what he was going to do, and he climbed out and jumped so quickly that they were unable to stop him. Starr saw them all go rushing down the stairs. When they told him what had happened, he was sure that the man must be dead, for he had fallen from five stories; but he heard afterwards that although most of his bones were broken he was still alive, and was taken to the hospital, where he died a little while afterwards.

After this terrible happening, which left everybody feeling rather bad for some time, all the windows of the top floor were fastened so that they could not be opened.

One day in May a party of women, who had been brought up from Fresnes and perhaps elsewhere, were assembled to wait for some time in the room that had been Ernest's. Starr went in to see them and gave them some chocolate that he had. "Pauline" and "Odette" were among them. Later they were taken away.[1]

[1] To Germany—in the first instance, to Karlsruhe. All of them were executed except "Odette," "Pauline" (Diana Rowden) at Natzweiler. See *The Natzweiler Trial* (William Hodge & Co.), Introduction.

Another day he saw his friend Maurice Southgate,[1] whom he had last encountered in Clermont Ferrand soon after his arrival in France. Their second meeting must also have been in May. It was in the late afternoon. Starr was sitting on a chair in his cell-workroom, the door open, and saw Southgate as he was going to the lavatory. A minute or two later Southgate came walking back, and, as he was facing Starr this time, saw him. They had known each other since they were boys — since Starr was twelve years old — their parents being friends and connected in business. Their eyes met; and as Southgate took in the picture — Starr at his ease smoking a cigarette and wearing a tie (which others did not), his door open — he paled.

Southgate was taken into the guardroom (Starr learned afterwards that he had been interrogated by Ernest during the whole of that day) and given something to lie down on for the night. Starr realized that to see him had been a shock to Maurice, and that he must do something about it. He couldn't very well explain loud enough for Southgate to hear him in the next room, but he whistled a few bars of *God Save the King*. Later, when they had a chance to speak, Maurice told him that he had been very thankful for the signal, which he had understood perfectly.

It was during the time when Southgate was being in-

---

[1] Squadron Leader Maurice Southgate, D.S.O., Légion d'Honneur, alias "Hector." Starr learned afterwards that he had already been a prisoner for about three weeks when he saw him.

terrogated that Ernest showed his photograph to Starr and asked if he knew the man. Starr said that he did not.

Ernest said, very likely bluffing, "Of course you know him! Because he knows you!"

Starr said, "If I know that man, my God, he's changed a lot, because I don't recognize that photo!"

Several days later the phone bell rang in the guard-room, and one of the guards called out, "It's for you, Starr!" It seemed very strange to be answering a phone after so many months. It was Ernest speaking, and he asked, "Have you had your lunch yet?"

"No."

"Well, if they bring it up, don't eat it, because you'll be having it with your cousin."

"My cousin? What are you talking about?"

"Yes. 'Hector,' Maurice Southgate. He *is* your cousin, isn't he?"

"Oh yes," he said, realizing that only Maurice could have said this, though for some reason that he could not fathom.

Kieffer's service had been aware of the activities of "Hector" for a long time and had been trying to catch him, but when Southgate was first arrested they had not realized that they had got their man. It was from Ernest's phone call that Starr learned that two and two had at last been put together.[1]

---

[1] When they met after the war Starr asked Southgate how it was that the Germans learned his code name. Southgate replied, "Well, at first I thought it was you who must have told them, but afterwards, in Buchenwald, I learned that it wasn't so." There a fellow prisoner

A little later he was taken down to the floor below, to a big room opposite Kieffer's where a table was laid for four — Ernest, Southgate, Starr and another whom he cannot remember.

During the meal the conversation ran only on generalities. Starr and Southgate talked to one another, but naturally said nothing significant with Ernest there. At one moment Kieffer came in, and coming up to Starr, said, "Bob, we ought to shoot you!"

"Why?"

"Because you knew perfectly well all the time who Hector was, and you didn't tell us."

"Well, did you expect me to?"

Kieffer answered after a very short pause, "No!" He exchanged a few words with Ernest and left.

The same day that he was identified, Southgate gave his word of honor not to escape. After this he slept in a cell on the premises, but, except when being interrogated, he spent most of his time in Starr's cell-cum-workroom. Here, to pass the time away, he would occasionally mend a chair or any other piece of furniture the Germans liked to bring in to him, for he was an interior decorator in civil life. At the same time his wireless operator, who had been captured with him and who had also given his parole, would amuse himself by fiddling with

---

had told him that one day at the Avenue Foch, after a long day's interrogation, he was being taken down the stairs when they met Ernest coming up. Ernest had said, "Do you know this man?" showing him a photograph of Southgate which he had in his hand. Taken off his guard, he had replied, "Yes. 'Hector.'"

broken wirelesses (ordinary receiving sets) and getting them to go again. Their own radios never worked for the Germans.

These two men were the only ones ever put in with Starr in this way. They were with him for some time, but although they spoke together, naturally they were careful and did not talk of what they had been doing in the field, and Starr did not think that a concealed microphone would have picked up anything of interest.

During the first day after Southgate's installation, Ernest gave Starr several maps of France on which he had to fill in, at Southgate's dictation, all the dumps and parachute grounds — somewhere around sixty or seventy — in "Hector's" area, pinpointing them with green dots. Ernest looked on all the while.

A day or two after this he saw Southgate being taken away and asked what they were going to do with him.

"Don't worry," they said. "He's going with Ernest and some others to the southwest of France and won't be back for a few days."

About a week later they returned; and Southgate and Starr were both shown photographs of Southgate in the car with the S.S. He had brought back quite a few personal belongings from his lodgings, which they had visited, but Starr never knew exactly what the purpose of the trip had been.[1]

One day, shortly after the discovery that "Hector"

[1]Ernest tells me that his trip with Southgate to Limoges, Tarbres and other places did not have the result he hoped.

was Maurice Southgate, Starr was escorted to Kieffer's office, and Kieffer fished out the very first map which he had copied and on which he had written No. 13, BOB. Kieffer showed him an area in the southwest and said, "Color that in and put HILAIRE." As he said this, he looked at Starr and said, "*Ihr Bruder*."

"My brother? I haven't got a brother in France."

Kieffer just continued to look at him fixedly and repeated, "*Ihr Bruder*."

This was how he first learned his brother's code name.

He asked, "Has this man you call my brother been arrested?"

"No."

By this time, the thirteen numbers on the map had grown into nearly thirty.

Maurice Southgate was still kept at the Avenue Foch for some time after this, and then to his regret was transferred elsewhere,[1] as they needed the cell he occupied at night for another prisoner.

Able to see the sun outside, and longing to breathe the fresh air, Starr suggested to Kieffer that they might be allowed to exercise sometimes in the courtyard below. Kieffer consented, and after that Starr and John were allowed to go down and walk round occasionally, under guard.

Later on, a big rectangle was dug out in this courtyard, lined with concrete and filled with water, thus making a reserve of static water which could be drawn from

---

[1] Southgate was later sent to Buchenwald; he returned alive.

in case of fire. Spring turned to summer, Starr's second in captivity. One evening, when it was stiflingly hot, especially up under the roof, Starr asked Kieffer if he would let him go for a swim in this "pool."

"That's a good idea!" said Kieffer. "We'll both go!"

He told two of the guards to come with them, and they all went down and looked at the water. Kieffer took off his coat, expanded his chest, stripped to his underwear and dived in in fine style, proceeding across the tank at a rapid crawl stroke. Starr plunged in after him, and they swam about together for some time, really enjoying it, while the S.S. guards, with perfectly straight faces, patrolled solemnly round and round the tank.

The day the Allies landed everybody was very grim. A few days later Starr was disappointed to see them all looking much brighter again. "We've got a new weapon!" they told him. "It's the V–1. We can bomb your cities without sending airplanes and one bomb is enough to wipe out a whole town. The south of England is now hidden by a pall of smoke."

They were, of course, too far behind the launching bases to see them going over, and had no idea what sort of weapon V–1 was. Kieffer thought it might be a kind of big gun, "A new Big Bertha, only better!"

Starr shook his head, and said he thought it was more likely a bomb with an engine and wings. Kieffer was very intrigued, and insisted on his drawing what he meant, asking all sorts of questions about its construction, as though Starr were an expert on the thing! Later, when no one was listening, Starr was able to get the B.B.C. and heard the word "doodlebug," which confirmed his idea that the weapon was something with an engine.

"We've razed London," Von Kapri told him after a day or two. "There's nothing left but rubble!"

"Impossible," said Starr.

"No; it's true. London has been burned down. The Führer says so."

"I still say it's impossible," replied Starr.

"Why?"

"You did it in 1940. The Führer said so! And you can't burn London twice."

But they assured him that they really had done it this time. "With the V–1."

"Oh!" he said. "You mean the doodlebugs?"

"The what?"

"The doodlebugs!" he repeated, and then rendered this word as well as he could in translation.

As the days passed, however, and it was plain that the V–1 was not holding up the process of the invasion, the Germans became very serious again. Starr kept quiet now, for they were anxious and short-tempered, and he judged that humor would not be appreciated.

It soon became evident that the Allies were pushing so far into the country that they would have to leave the Avenue Foch and retire to an H.Q. in a town further back.

Now began a period of hurried activity. Prisoners began to be sent away.[1] Papers had to be either destroyed or packed up. Everybody was packing things.

Kieffer came to see Starr, and told him he was being sent to Buchenwald.

A little while afterwards, one Rühl, a man from the radio department, who had come up to the top floor for something, spoke to him. "Now that you're going," he said, "there's something I think you ought to know. Kieffer three times received an order from Berlin to have you shot, and each time he refused to comply with it.[2] Now I am very glad to hear that you are being sent to a concentration camp." It might seem strange to receive congratulations on being sent to a concentration camp, but Rühl either can have had no idea what conditions were like or thought that at any rate Starr would stand a chance of surviving. Certainly his congratulations were sincere.

[1] John had been sent away some time before, though Starr could not say in what month. He was later executed (shot) at Mauthausen.
[2] This was confirmed after the war when Starr spoke to French police officials at the Surveillance du Territoire in Paris.

VI
Sachsenhausen

OWING TO THE dislocation of communications, the train in which he traveled with some other prisoners took eight days to get from Paris to Saarbrücken, where they were kept for a fortnight. Then they were transferred to another train, which was to take them to Buchenwald.

About a hundred and twenty of them were packed into a car, and as there was not room for all of them to lie down, or even sit, at the same time, they had to take turns. They were each given a piece of bread when they started, but during the four days and four nights that the journey lasted they were not given any more food or drink, and the carriages were not opened (except on one occasion) for any purpose. The conditions inside were soon indescribable. It must have been August, and was very hot. There was a big tin in one corner, but it was nowhere near adequate for the number of men, and after a little time was overflowing.

As if by instinct, the inhabitants of the car had divided themselves into two groups, Russians and East Europeans in the first and other nationalties in the second — Starr had palled up with some Frenchmen. The

Russians did not mind the overflow from the tin as much as the rest, and indeed, availing themselves of the space created because other people did not want to stand on that part of the floor, lay down on it to sleep.

One night the German guards pushed them all over on one side to count them, and found one missing. They declared that a Pole had escaped. How this could be was a mystery. Starr believed that he must have been missing from before they started, since there was no means of egress perceptible to those still inside.

To punish them for the escape, the guards opened the door and showed them big cans of macaroni soup, and of water, which apparently they were bringing round to the other carriages, and said, "None of it's for you!" About half an hour later, however, the doors were opened again, and a big can was shoved in with a few noodles left in it. There was a frenzied rush on the part of the few men who felt tempted by this stuff, and they dived in, fighting like demons. Soon there were bits of noodles in their hair, and they were picking it off each other and even off the floor, where it was already mixing with the filth. Although it was a horrible sight, Starr and the little group of prisoners who had now become his friends could not help laughing, and whenever they met again (in concentration camp) it was rarely that they did not refer to "*la bataille des nouilles,*" the battle of the noodles.

When the train reached the railway station where they should have been taken out for Buchenwald, they remained in it for two or three hours. Somehow word came through that the authorities had refused to accept them because the camp was full, and that after discussion it had been decided to take them somewhere else. The train moved on again and they wondered where they were going.

They got out finally at Sachsenhausen, in the Berlin area, and marched into Sachsenhausen Concentration Camp. Here they were taken into a big hut, filled with benches, and kept waiting for some hours. They all clamored for food and water, especially water, which they had not tasted since they set out on their journey from Saarbrücken, but none seemed immediately to be forthcoming. Some of them, Starr among them, could not resist the temptation to drink from a tap they could see, although the guards told them the water was not good. This resulted some days later in a touch of dysentery, though, as Starr had drunk very little of the water, he was not ill enough for it to be noticeable.

Eventually the guards did bring round bowls of soup, so-called, and when they had drunk it they were marched out and lined up in front of the delousing hut. Here they formed part of a queue of some two or three thousand. Presently he could hear a voice inquiring, or rather yelling, down the long line, "*Wo ist der Engländer?*" ("Where is the Englishman?")

It was an S.S. man, and he worked his way up the queue, repeating all the time, "*Wo ist der Engländer?*"

Starr said, "Here!"

The S.S. man called to him to come out of the ranks, and shouted, "Attention!"

Starr remained standing in the position that suited him, which was somewhat slouched.

The S.S. man demanded, "Are you a parachutist?"

"Yes."

"Is that how British parachute men stand at attention?"

"No. Not when they are on parade in their own country."

The S.S. man began to kick him. He could hear friendly voices calling out, *"Ne t'en fais pas, mon vieux!"*

Eventually his part of the queue got into the hut. Here their names were checked and they were given numbers, by which they were henceforth known. Then they were relieved of any valuables they had on them, stripped, and marched into a series of rooms, where they were successively shaved from head to foot, sent under a shower, disinfected, and issued a thin suit of striped prison garments. Finally, they came out of the hut on the other side to be paraded.

Here they had to start looking round to try to find their friends again. Men who had come in, many of them, with long hair and fuzzy beards looked so different, completely hairless as they were, that they peered uncertainly into each other's faces in search of a familiar feature, saying, "I'm So-and-so. Who are you?" In spite of everything, they were nearly all laughing by this time.

Then they were taken and put in their huts. So far as Starr can remember, his was Block 49.

These huts were under the supervision of prisoners, many of them Germans, either political or "common law" prisoners; in the latter case they were serving sentences for such crimes as murder, or any others punishable by life imprisonment. Most of these block chiefs had been in the camp for more than ten years, never going out at all. Pretty tough, they were nevertheless not so bad as the S.S. to have anything to do with.

The hut was divided into three sections; in the middle were the block chief, his second in command and the block secretary, who did the bookkeeping, kept the lists of prisoners, and so on, and some other helpers; and on either side were the remainder of the prisoners, roughly about eight hundred men in each section. One of the sections was directly under the supervision of the block chief, the other of his second in command. The prisoners were sleeping two or three to a bunk, as the camp had become very overcrowded.

Early in the morning on the day after they had been installed in their block, they were paraded for roll call and lined up in groups of five. The block chief handed a list to the S.S. man who was in charge of several blocks, and they began to pass down the lines together, the S.S. man counting them aloud, five by five. Sometimes he would think he might have made a mistake, and go back a few groups and count them again to make sure.

When he had finally counted them, he asked, "*Wo ist der Engländer?*"

Starr said, "Here."

The S.S. man, who was tall and thin, beckoned to him to come out of the rank and stand in front of him, looked him up and down and said, "*Du bist nicht so lang für einen Engländer!*" ("You are not so tall for an Englishman!")

Starr looked him up and down in the same way, and said, "*Ja, und du bist nicht so fett für einen Deutscher!*" ("And you're not so fat for a German!")

The S.S. man looked at him with a rather strange expression, and after a few seconds stretched out his hand and made him a sign to go back into the rank. This mild reaction did not surprise Starr, as he had learned already that a little cheek was more likely than anything to gain respect.

As soon as the S.S. man had disappeared from sight, the block chief beckoned to him. "*Tommy! Komm hier!*" He took Starr to the entrance of the hut, made him wait there, went in and came back with a suit of warm clothes. They were civilian clothes, although in the back of the jacket a big hole had been cut out and filled up with a very obvious patch.

That evening, just as they were going to retire to their bunks, the chief came in, beckoned to him, and asked him if he could write. (The camp was very largely filled with East Europeans, and apparently many of the prisoners were illiterates.) When Starr replied that he could, he was then taken into the "staff" section in the middle, where he was told to sit down at a big table with two or three others, and until quite late that night they were filling in new cards to help the block secretary. During these proceedings, they were provided with a little extra food and a cigarette.

Shortly after this they were all paraded one morning on the Appellplatz. Their numbers were called out, and each man was notified to which work command he was appointed. When Starr's number was called, he was allotted a command which he had heard given to none of the others. It was the Strafe Kommando. This was the punishment command, to which prisoners were sent when they had offended in one way or another.

He had a visit from some Norwegians, who had heard that an Englishman had arrived, and when they had seen him and made sure that this was true, they went away and came back with some other Englishmen. These were all naval men, one of them a lieutenant, who had been captured together while doing a commando job in Norway. (To the best of his knowledge, he was the only member of S.O.E. in Sachsenhausen.) They lived in the Strafe Block, and had been on the Strafe Kommando for about a year and a half, if he remembers rightly.

The morning after the distribution of work, he had to report to the Strafe Block and was given a pair of new boots and something to wrap round his feet. Then he had to fall in with the Strafe Kommando, and they

were marched away from the hut to the Appellplatz, and
when they got there they began marching in step round
it. It lay between the lines of huts, and the building
over the entrance was occupied by German office
staff.

The Appellplatz was a piece of ground in the shape of
a semicircle. Round the circumference shallow pits had
been dug out and filled in with various materials, one
with sand, one with cobblestones, one with loose stones
and flints, and another with water, the idea being to
reproduce all the conditions that one might encounter
while marching. Round this they marched from six in
the morning to six at night, covering nearly thirty-five
miles a day, with occasional halts while a man in civilian clothes would come and inspect their boots and take
notes. They were testing *ersatz* leather for the Wehrmacht. For a man who had not walked for more than
a year, it was pretty grim. The British prisoners calculated that since they had arrived they must have
marched the distance from Berlin to New York, from
New York back to Berlin, and halfway across the Atlan-
tic again.

The chief of the Strafe Block was a German called
Jakob. He was a big brute of a man and usually kicked
people when he came round to see them. Starr discovered that he could kick extremely hard. Nevertheless,
he possessed a heart still capable of being reached on
occasions. If Starr remembers his story rightly, he had
deserted from the Wehrmacht in order to visit his wife

and children and had been sentenced for life; but Starr would not like to vouch for this history.

Although expecting to be transferred to the Strafe Block now that he worked with the Strafe Kommando, Starr returned for the time being to his old block every night. It happened that the block secretary was called somewhere else for a few days, and Starr was given his job of maintaining guard over the entrance to the hut while the prisoners' roll call was taken. Being tired and bored, he looked one day into the hut behind him and saw an electric fire with a plate of soup keeping warm underneath it, a chair, and a book on a table. So he went in, sat down and began looking at the book. He could hear the muster being taken, and thought it would be time enough to return to his post when it got near the end.

Engrossed in examining the book, he became suddenly aware, out of the corner of his eye, of a glint of greenish uniform, and realized that two S.S. had loomed into the doorway. He was so startled that he leaped out of the chair, and for the first time since his captivity stood perfectly at attention. One of them was the thin man he had said was not so fat. This one, smiling for once in his life, exclaimed, "*So! Gut, Tommy, gut!*" and motioned him to resume the chair.

The regular camp rations, weak soup, bread and sausage, were so insufficient that the prisoners would hardly have kept alive if it had not been that the Norwegians, alone of all the nationalities, were allowed to receive food parcels, like ordinary P.O.Ws., and shared these with the English. The English, who were all in the Strafe Block, shared these gifts with the other nationalities in the same command, and Starr, of course, shared his with some of the inmates of Block 49. In fact, the Norwegians probably gave away more than they kept for themselves.

After about ten days on the Strafe Kommando, Starr was told that he would be transferred to the Strafe Block at the end of the second week. Just before the end of this week, however, typhus broke out in Block 49, and he was unable to go as they were all in quarantine.

Now having nothing to do, he reverted to art. The prisoners all wore white cotton rectangles on their clothes on which were printed in black the first letter of their nationality, and their number beside it in red. He found the place where the paint was kept, and started to decorate the hut.

With the two colors he could make an effective design; he drew trees with red trunks and black foliage, or vice versa, hills, valleys, waterfalls, bridges, castles, villages with churches and cottages, wonderful landscapes running all round the room. On one wall he did a view of Nuremberg, magnified and elaborated from a picture postcard someone produced.

When at last the typhus was over, the block chief decided that it was not necessary for Starr to go on testing leather for the Wehrmacht, and kept him instead for drawing murals in another hut. From now on he was drawing all the time, as hut after hut had to be decorated. The chief of the Norwegians' block made him come and do his room.

It was interesting to Starr to notice how, although they had all come into the camp on terms as equal as any men could be — naked, without possessions, and even without names — a society had developed as differentiated and complicated as any in the world. As soon as men had been in for a little time they began to find their level and to sort themselves out according to capacities and affinities, the cleverer inevitably managing to get themselves advantages. Indeed, it was soon clear that he was still in a hierarchized world. As by one means and another people became possessed of things, mainly extracted from materials given them by the Germans to work with, a highly complex system of trade had developed, which was carried on by means of barter. Among so many men were naturally some drawn from almost every occupation — mechanics, carpenters, craftsmen, electricians, scientists, tailors, and so on. Somebody was producing beautiful little cigarette holders made partly from cables and partly from the windscreens of Heinkels. The materials were arranged in decorative bands, and bore very little signs of amateur work. Some were making electric stoves, adapted both for heating and for cooking, and it was one of them that the block chief had in his room. Indeed, not only was there a diversity of employments (apart from those prescribed by the Germans): there were soon richer and poorer. It depended on the ingenuity with which a man could adapt the materials that came to his hand, or with which he could trade them. Again, if he could not, in the commands to which he was allotted, obtain materials, he could sell whatever skill he might have.

There was one man who was producing round, close-fitting caps from some fabric which he had got hold of. Autumn was drawing on to winter now, and everybody's head felt cold, so he did a considerable business. Starr purchased one for two tins of sardines. He was doing quite well, and the civilian suit given him on the first evening gained him a certain prestige.

People made friends and went visiting each other, as in any other society. Starr and the Frenchmen with whom he had traveled in the truck from Saarbrücken soon found one another's quarters, and would meet for a chat and to exchange reminiscences and new experiences. Sometimes he was able to make up a parcel of food for them.

Stuck here and there round the walls of the camp were wirelesses with loud-speakers, so there was always something to hear.

For weeks before Christmas everybody was preparing for the occasion and making things, determined to celebrate the festival with all the traditional rites that they could manage. The Norwegians made a tremendous showing, and on Christmas Eve their huts were magnificently gay with paper and other decorations most ingeniously and imaginatively put together. Right in the middle of the Appellplatz appeared an enormous Christmas tree, festooned with illuminations shining through colored glass. Starr did not know where this had come from.

New Year's Day passed, and January gave way to February.

One night they heard shots being fired and wondered what had happened. Next morning Starr went over to the Strafe Block to see his English friends and found that they had all disappeared. He asked the others what had happened to them; but although they all looked extremely unhappy, he could not get a square answer out of any of them, so he asked Jakob, the Strafe Block chief.

Jakob, although usually such a bully, was so distressed that at first he could neither look at Starr nor answer him. At last, when he had got control of his voice, he told Starr that they had been taken away and hanged from hooks on the wall. It was evident that he was deeply ashamed. He said it was a terrible thing to take prisoners and hang them; that it was murder and a disgrace to Germany. He said this so loud that anyone passing might have heard him. The English, he said, had been good boys, all of them. He was not only cursing, as he said all this, he was even weeping. Putting his hand on Starr's arm, he said, "Luckily, you were not in the Strafe Block last night, but I'm afraid they will come again for you."

It seemed probable that the order had come through to liquidate all the British, and that Starr had been missed only because he had not been with the others. Everybody seemed to think that he would be fetched the following morning, at the same time as the others had been. In spite of it all, he was able to sleep that night. When he woke in the morning he found that friends were waiting to say good-by to him, so he sat up on the edge of his bunk and shook hands with them all in turn. Everyone tried to say something consoling or encouraging.

With part of his mind he was conscious of this as a theatrical scene, which somehow lacked reality, and could almost see himself holding court, "showing off and being brave." This was because, in spite of everything, he could not feel inside that his time had come. He felt sure, against all logic, that something would happen to save him. Nevertheless, he did give to one of the Norwegians a pipe cleaner and a cigarette holder which he had, and asked him to send it to Michelle after the war as a little souvenir.

Presently the chief of Block 49 came to tell him that a chit had just been received in the office saying that he was to be kept under observation in the Strafe Block. As the morning wore on, it became evident that an enormous evacuation of prisoners was taking place. Hundreds were being massed to march out.

Suddenly Jakob came to find him, very excited, and led him toward the crowd of men. "Slip yourself into that column," he said. "This place is no good to you!"

Starr did not know, and neither, probably, did Jakob, that this column of prisoners was going to an extermination camp.[1]

[1] *Vernichtungslager.*

VII

Mauthausen

THEY WERE NOW counted five by five and marched to
a railway siding, where a train composed of cattle cars
was waiting for them. They were packed in, and so
began a journey that was to last three days and three
nights. The general conditions were much the same as
in the train which had brought Starr from Saarbrücken
to Sachsenhausen, though on the whole not quite so bad,
as they were given a little food and water occasionally
and the cars were open at the top so that they had air.
Nevertheless, more than a third of the prisoners died
before they were taken out of the train.[1]

Near the end of their journey they crossed the frontier
into Austria, and for a few miles followed the Danube
through snow-covered mountains.

When they got out at Mauthausen,[2] on February 17,
1945, they were marched through the streets of the town.
The people were so ashamed that they could not look
at them. Some of the women were crying, and the men
turned away.

[1] According to an article entitled "La Nuit du 17 Février," which
appeared in the postwar *Information and Liaison Bulletin* of the ex-
prisoners of Mauthausen (February 1946), out of 2500 who left
Sachsenhausen by this convoy 1700 only arrived at Mauthausen alive.
[2] About twenty miles beyond Linz.

Following a road that led, if Starr remembers rightly, somewhat above the town, they came to a place with massive walls made with big stone blocks. He supposed this was it. As they approached the entrance they could see in big letters above the gate the words: DU KOMMST NIEMALS RAUS (YOU NEVER COME OUT).

They were brought into the camp, lined up on parade, and told that any who were sick should stand to one side. Starr had a premonition that those who did so were going to be killed. Many, however, did as they were told, believing that they were going to receive medical treatment. Starr heard an S.S. say to one who stepped out, *"Du gehst nach Hause!"* ("You're going home!")

He learned later that they were all exterminated.

After the sick had been taken away, those who remained were counted again, and Starr made out, from what he could understand of the conversation between the S.S., that they were discussing how many of the new arrivals they could cope with, and how many, in addition to those who had gone already, they should exterminate.[1]

They were kept hanging about for an hour or two, then marched to the back of the cookhouse, where they were told to strip off all their clothes, which were taken away from them. Shivering in the bitter cold, they were kept waiting, in the open, for perhaps another couple of hours, until nightfall. There was snow on the ground.

---

[1] According to the article cited, about two hundred had reported sick and been sent for extermination; it was, however, desired to reduce the number by four hundred, and so it was decided to bring the deaths up to this figure.

Then they were herded in groups into a shower bath.

Here they were paraded before two or three doctors, or so-called doctors, who looked them over like cattle, felt their backs, and marked them, with an indelible pencil, either with a number written on the chest or else with a K between the shoulder blades, just where it was difficult to rub off. Starr was given a number on the chest.

He now found himself in a group which had to wait for some time. They were then shaved from head to foot and treated with disinfectant sloshed on with a huge brush. It stung and burned like fury, and for some minutes afterwards they looked like men possessed with St. Vitus's dance.

Now the whole lot were whipped back into the shower baths, which were by this time filled with steam so that they soon ran perspiration from every pore. The guards lashed them with sprays of scalding hot water, which was practically unbearable, and then with glacial cold. After about half an hour of this treatment they were turned outside to stand once more, still naked, in the snow and biting night wind.

After an interval they were collected and beaten back into the shower hut once more and the whole process began again. Starr cannot remember with certainty whether he was put through the procedure twice or three times.

Eventually the fortunate and the unfortunate were separated. Those who had got a K on their backs were destined to continue to be put through the showers, again and again, until the early hours of the morning, after which they were made to run about in the open. Anyone who fell was immediately killed. This went on until they were all dead save one Frenchman who escaped the final blow.

Starr was given a thin pair of trunks and taken out into the open again. After hanging around for some time, he was, with various others, taken to a block of buildings that were still in the course of construction. There were neither windows nor doors, though there were the gaps for them; and the floor was cement. Here they were required to give their names, nationalities, and so on, and Starr, by force of habit, said British, which he afterwards realized was the most foolish thing he could have done.[1] They were then taken down to the basement and left to sleep on the beaten earth. As they were freezing cold, they all crept together to get a little warmth. After a very short while it was not just earth they were lying on. The cans provided were, as always, hopelessly inadequate, and this time the overflow soon covered the whole floor.

For three days they were kept in this place, only coming out for the roll call, which would last from about three to six each morning, during which they would have to stand in ranks, and a thin pair of trunks did not afford much protection against the climate.

[1] To the best of his knowledge, he was the only Englishman in Mauthausen while he was there.

Then they were put into a hut and told to sit down
cross-legged, in rows. Once they were arranged like this
they could not sit in any other way as they were packed
so tight. Here they were kept for a few days, always
sitting in the same position except for roll calls and so on.
Then they were taken and separated into groups, and
distributed among various huts in different parts of the
camp.

Starr was among those sent to No. 3 Camp, which
consisted of about eight tumbledown huts put up on
muddy ground in the lower part of the whole camp, and
surrounded by big stone walls. The huts were not of the
usual type, divided into compartments, but were one-
roomed affairs, without tables, benches or bunks. Apart
from a pile of dirty and half-empty palliasses at one end
and a pile or two of blankets, there was nothing.

By this time they had been allocated a thin pair of
trousers and a jacket each, but were still barefooted. A
few pairs of boots, belonging to the huts and not to any
individual, had always to be left outside, so that every
morning about twelve hundred men would have to fight
over about two hundred boots. During the day they
would stand around outside the huts, if the sun was shining, or gather together in groups of about fifty or a
hundred, leaning up against each other, trying to keep
a little warm.

At nightfall the palliasses were laid on the floor, and
as each man entered the hut he had to lie down beside
the previous prisoner, his head to the other's feet, so that

they would take up less room than if all the heads had been the same way. With more than a thousand men to get into the hut, there was not an inch to spare. They were packed, literally, like sardines.

Blankets were then laid over them, one over about four men. It was virtually impossible to move a hairsbreadth all night long. As much as anything in Mauthausen, Starr disliked this lying with his face at somebody's feet — the feet, perhaps, of a dying man who would be a corpse before daybreak.

In the morning there would be a roll call outside the hut and they would be lined up as usual, five by five. So that the S.S. could always count the correct number they had, when they got up, to bring the dead out with them and lay them out, five by five also.

This went on day after day. They were given in the morning bowls of what was called "coffee" but was in fact tepid water with a peculiar taste. Later on each was doled out a piece of black bread, exactly the sixteenth part of a loaf and about the size of a packet of twenty cigarettes. This "bread" was so moldy that sometimes it would already have disintegrated, and they would be issued a handful of crumbs. All they had later in the day was a ladleful of soup, so-called, and if they found in it a potato peel or a bean they considered themselves lucky. Once a week they had a little slice of sausage and a piece of margarine about as big as four lumps of sugar.

If the daily piles of dead were considered insufficient, then there would be a gas-chamber parade, this happening perhaps once a fortnight. The occupants of the hut would be lined up outside, and a man would come along the ranks, feel the biceps of each prisoner, and make his selection according to weakness.

Mauthausen, Starr learned, was used as a *Strafe* camp (punishment camp) to which prisoners from ordinary concentration camps like Buchenwald or Sachsenhausen were sent if they had committed some offense or been found unmanageable. Men arriving from Buchenwald, Dachau, and even from Auschwitz, which was, like Mauthausen, an extermination camp, would speak regretfully of "the good days" in the places they had left — without irony, because in comparison with Mauthausen they were remembered as good places.

Every day about twelve men would go to fetch the soup cans. On the way they would pass in front of the incinerators, where it would be a common sight to see a wooden truck of corpses drawn up and the bodies pitched down a chute into the furnace, and then the gas chamber, where one might see a queue of the doomed going in.

The return journey with the soup was hazardous. It had to be brought back in enormous cans, which the prisoners carried one on either side, generally followed by maurauding prisoners from other huts. If they were not sufficiently protected, the men who were following them (nearly always the Russians) would attack the convoy, overturn the cans and begin scooping and licking the soup from the ground.

Even when they had got it "home" safely the danger was not over, since a hut where the soup had arrived was generally invaded. In Starr's hut, where the morale was still civilized, they organized the defense of the meal. The twenty judged to be the stoutest, of whom Starr was one, would delay their own meal until after the others had finished and form a cordon round them, facing outwards and armed with sticks. The Russians would circle round them, menacing, with their enormous hungry eyes staring, as they sought for a weak man whose food they could steal. Starr, a permanent member of the cordon, will never forget their expressions.

The members of the cordon, when it came to their turn to have their "food," ate — or rather drank — as quickly as possible, bent very low over it, so as not to lose it. Altogether, mealtimes at Mauthausen were times of extreme tension, and there was nearly always hand-to-hand fighting with the robbers.

At a later period of his stay in Mauthausen, No. 3 Camp was evacuated and the former inhabitants dispersed among huts elsewhere in the camp. Other groups of prisoners were marched into No. 3 Camp to take their places, and as soon as these had entered, the gates were locked on them and they were left to starve. Some time afterwards, Starr was one of a small party sent back into No. 3 Camp to fetch some boots, and there it was that he saw two living skeletons fighting literally over a blade of grass.

From the part of the camp where he was now he could

always see the gas chamber, which took in regularly a huge number, believed in the camp to be five hundred, every twenty-four hours, the bodies being passed afterwards by an internal channel into the adjoining incinerator.

At any time of the day one might see the queue going in, which it did by a rather circuitous route, winding round several places, and it was a strange thing to Starr to see how patiently they went in. He never saw anyone try to break out of the queue, although there were very few guards supervising its slow progress, and it seemed to him that the desire for life had become extinct.

He decided that if his number were called he would resist — better to die fighting than go in with the queue.

He used to dream a great deal all the time he was in Mauthausen. One night he dreamed that he was swimming, pursued by something he cannot remember. The water was so transparent that he could see and count all the little fishes and the pebbles at the bottom. After this he got out, went up a bank, out through a gate, and slammed it behind him.

This dream was so vivid that he told the block secretary about it, who said that he knew a man who interpreted dreams. This prisoner listened to his dream, and said, very quietly, "You're one of the few people who are going to get out of here alive. You'll be among the first to leave and you won't have to do anything much about it yourself. You'll find it will just happen."

Even with death all around him, he still never at any time really believed that he was going to die himself. He had always had in the back of his mind something that had been told him by a friend of his mother's whom he had seen when he was about eighteen. She had noticed that on both his hands his life line stopped short, but that on the right hand there appeared at a point corresponding to its termination a substitute line, in the form of a branch from the fate line. She had said, "The left hand is what you come into the world with, but the right is what you make yourself," and had gone on to explain that he would at some point in his life pass through experiences so dreadful that they should by rights kill him, but that he would live by virtue of his sheer will to do so. In Mauthausen, it seemed to him that the conditions for making good this prophecy had been realized. He had faith. It was largely the prophecy that had given him faith. And he was sure that it was faith that kept him alive.

He came to believe, in fact, that, barring murder, the factor which determined whether one lived or died was moral. If he saw a man sitting with his head between his knees, declaring that they would none of them ever get out and that they would all die there, after a little time he would find that the man had died. On the other hand, many who were physically weaker would keep on going because they had not given up hope.

Some time during this period a number of women prisoners arrived in Mauthausen and were put in No. 2 Camp.

The camp as a whole was set on a slope, so that they could see a little over the top of the walls and look at a line of snow-covered mountains visible in the distance. Spring came, and grass appeared as the snow began to melt on the lower slopes.

Then one day strange news arrived — that there were some Swiss Red Cross trucks outside the camp, and that they were taking away the women and a few French and Belgian men to fill up any space left, and would be coming back afterwards for the rest of the Frenchmen and Belgians. At first the men could hardly credit such a thing. But sure enough, the women were evacuated, and Frenchmen and Belgians with them. After this, while the camp was buzzing with excitement and speculation, some of the Frenchmen came to see Starr and told him that he had now the chance to leave Mauthausen. They said they would have his card at the office, where some of them worked, torn up, and a new one made out for him as a Frenchman. He decided to keep the name Starr, but to have them put Jean instead of John. They also changed for him the metal identity disc which he wore like the rest of them — bearing his number and nationality and the word MAUTHAUSEN — attached to a bracelet round his wrist.

It was now up to him to pass through this transformation unnoticed, and he decided to take into his confidence the block chief, who was a Pole, so that the latter should not make a blunder and give him away when the day arrived and his number was called out as a Frenchman. The Pole agreed to be silent, but he said, "When you do get back, don't forget to let the world know what went on here. Don't ever forget, and try not to let others forget."

The big day arrived, and when lists of the French and Belgian prisoners were handed in to the block chief, with orders that these men were to be paraded in the morning in front of the offices hut, STARR, JEAN, was on the list. His first reaction was one of immense joy; at last he was going to be free and to return home again. Then all of a sudden he was terribly afraid; in fact, it was the first time he really knew what fear was. Because freedom was so near now, he could feel himself trembling inside. All through that day — they did not leave until nightfall — he did not know how he managed to hold himself together. He kept thinking that something might go wrong. He felt that it was his day of destiny, either death or liberty.

Eventually they were assembled and a roll call taken. He saw the block chief looking for him, as he came down the lines, anxious to see whether he had managed it. When he spotted Starr, he gave him a glint with his eyes. After the roll call had been taken they were marched to the gates, and as they went through them he thought that they had passed through the final stage.

Then he saw that there was still another hut, outside the

walls, of which he had known nothing. Now he was trembling so much that he could hardly control himself.

While they were lining up in front of the second hut, which appeared to be an office, a man whom he recognized as having been formerly the chief prisoner of Sachsenhausen, but who was now in S.S. uniform, came up to meet them. As he drew up to their group he recognized Starr and said, "But you're not a Frenchman — you are English," and looked for a moment as though he were going to denounce him.

"Yes," Starr replied. "But in a very short while now the war will be over, and you can help yourself best now by saying nothing, and maybe I could put in a good word for you."

The man answered nothing and let him pass.

They were marched into the hut ten by ten and went up in turn to an N.C.O., who was checking up names and numbers in a big card index and giving some particulars about each one to a secretary who was sitting typing at a table beside him. When he saw this extra check on their identities, which no one had foreseen, Starr's heart sank. After he had found the card corresponding to each prisoner, the N.C.O. asked him whether he had had any money, watch or other valuables when he entered the camp. This appeared to be a formality, as, although he took note of the answers, Starr never saw anything returned.

When his turn came the man started looking through the cards, and having gone right through them without finding STARR, JEAN, started looking through them from the beginning again.

Starr said, to help it through, "*Ich habe kein Geld. Keine Uhr. Nichts.*" ("I have no money. No watch. Nothing.") The man made a sign as if to say, "Be quiet," and went on fumbling with the cards. Then suddenly he lost patience and made a gesture with his arm. "Get along!"

Starr passed through into another room, where he was given a moderately clean suit, shirt, tie, shoes and hat.

Then they were marched back through the big gates again into the camp, where they waited till evening, a further torment to Starr. At times the camp commander and other officials came up and looked at them very carefully from head to foot.

Then at last they were marched through the gates again and down to the waiting trucks.

As they drew away from Mauthausen, from every truck and from every mouth there burst the "Marseillaise."

2

They passed through the town of Linz and spent the night in a huge farmyard loft. The second night, still in Austria, they stayed at an inn. At every place where they stopped the people came out of their houses to bring them everything they could to eat, and the innkeeper must have brought them his entire stock.

On the third day they arrived at the Swiss border. In Switzerland they were driven first to a hospital, where their clothes were taken off and put through a disinfecting process and they themselves were given a shower, hot and cold (but not as at Mauthausen, though it brought back memories). Any of the men who seemed to be in the least overcome by the shower were kept at the hospital, the others being taken to the local schoolroom, where they slept the night in a pile of straw. Next day they were taken to Zürich (or Bern), where they were again put in a schoolroom, always guarded by Swiss guards. During the day the Swiss people came out and threw packets of chocolate and cigarettes to them through the open windows.

Later, a lady from the Belgian consulate came to take the names of the Belgians who were there. Although it was practically the end of the war, they still had to be interned, temporarily at least. Starr spoke to this lady, gave her his identity, and asked her if she would get in touch with the British authorities, let them know that he was in Switzerland and ask them what he should do.[1] Before they left this place, she told him that he had been instructed to stay with the French until they had left Switzerland — in other words, he must remain French.

While they were here, they were issued such clothes as the Swiss Red Cross could muster for them. Starr got

---

[1] The message having reached London, Michelle received a telegram from Miss Atkins: PLEASED TO INFORM YOU YOUR HUSBAND SAFE AWAITING REPATRIATION. It arrived on the afternoon of V.E. Day itself. Michelle had never given up hope.

a pair of blue plus fours made for a schoolboy, a checked brown and white waistcoat, striped socks, and brown and white shoes with very pointed toes that turned up.

They were then transferred to a camp outside Geneva, and after several days taken by train to France.

When they had crossed the frontier and arrived at the first French station, the municipal band, which was waiting on the platform to welcome them, struck up the "Marseillaise." Afterwards the people who had assembled rushed forward to give them a tremendous welcome, passing up eggs, butter, milk, wine and everything imaginable through the carriage windows. Then came the pathetic scene of mothers and wives showing photographs of their boys and husbands and asking the men in the train for any possible news.

After a while the train pulled out, and took them on a little farther to a place where they were taken to a repatriation camp. Here identities were checked, and after spending a night in the camp Starr was sent on with a trainload of men who were going to Paris. At each station where the train stopped people would be waiting to meet them, and there would be the same scenes as at the frontier station. When they got to Dijon, Starr, still mindful of any events that might have followed his capture, and hoping that intelligence of his arrest had reached his colleagues quickly, asked some of the people who came to greet them whether they had ever heard of a man who had tried to escape from the prison in

July 1943 and been wounded while running down the
street. "Oh, yes!" they assured him. "We all heard about
that!" This was a great satisfaction to him.

When they arrived in Paris there was another identity
check, and like the others he was given a special identity
card, some money and a parcel. They asked him whether
he had somewhere to go. He wanted more than anything
now to be alone, in order to have the sensation of complete freedom, and said, "You don't have to put me up.
I have an apartment in Paris."

He arrived at his flat in Issy-les-Moulineaux at about
5 A.M. The concierge and his wife got up immediately,
put the coffee pot on the stove, and talked till breakfast
time.

At about nine o'clock he left them and went to the
office where he had worked before the war, the Agence
Yves Alexandre Publicité. They did not recognize him
immediately, but when they did they gave him a great
welcome. He next reported to the Military Attaché's
office in Paris and was told to go to the Hotel Bristol,
which was a hotel for British officers. When he entered
the bar his appearance caused some astonishment, and
one of the officers there asked, "Who are you?"

"I've just come from Mauthausen extermination
camp," he said.

Then they were all around him in a minute, plying
him with questions.

During the morning an Intelligence Corps man came
to check up on his identity, and when this had been

done he was given some money and papers, so that he could go and get himself dressed and equipped once more as a British officer.

It was V.E. Day itself and the whole city was in a state of the most ecstatic celebration, people singing and dancing everywhere they went. To Starr, completely in a daze, it seemed almost unreal; he could hardly believe it, and he hardly knew what world he was in.

The next afternoon he was driven out to Le Bourget, having been given a priority trip back to England. When he arrived, the plane was full up. The pilot, who was standing at the door, said, "I'm sorry, old chap; all the seats are taken. You'll have to sit on the luggage in the tail."

He thought he would probably be sick if he was dumped there, and was feeling so tired and worn out that he said, "I don't think I could stand that trip. I've just come out of an extermination camp, and don't feel any too strong."

"You've come from *where?*"

"From Mauthausen extermination camp."

"Follow me! You're our guest!"

The pilot took him right up to the front of the plane, told him to sit on a little seat just behind the cockpit, and said, "Sit there till we take off. Then you can come and sit up in front." And in fact, as soon as they were airborne, he took the copilot's seat.

It was a clear bright day, and while they were still out over the channel, just at the moment when the thin line of the white cliffs of England came into view, the B.B.C. (to which he was listening through the earphones they had given him) struck up "God Save the King."

He was crying like a baby.

VIII

Homecoming

THE PLANE LANDED at Croydon Aerodrome, where, after going with the others through the usual formalities, he was told to wait a while. Presently two men arrived with a little truck and said, "We've come to fetch you."

He naturally thought they were going to drive into London, and that they had been sent by the French Section to take him to their old H.Q., and therefore did not even ask where they were going. But as they drove on, and seemed to be going more and more into the country, he asked, "Here! Where are we going?"

"We're going to a place near Guildford."

"Guildford! What on earth for? That's where we started from, isn't it?" (Wanborough Manor was near Guildford.)

"Yes. We've been given orders to pick you up and take you there."

He was a bit put out, as he had been hoping to go home almost immediately. However, if there were more formalities to go through, he supposed he would have to put up with it.

In due course they arrived at what would have been in any other circumstances a very charming country house, and he reported to the C.O. and asked how long he would have to stay here before being allowed to proceed home.

"Probably not long. It's just a matter of formality."

After waiting for a day or two, during which nothing happened, an officer came down from the War Office, and said that he would have to write out a report of everything that had happened since he was infiltrated into France.

"But that will take a long time, and I want to go home!"

"Sorry, but it will have to be done," said the officer, and left.

The next morning he said to the C.O., "I don't mind writing out a rough outline, but that's all I intend to do before I've been home. If you want to keep me here you'll have to guard the place, and pretty well, because I've got out of places belonging to the Gestapo. If you don't give me leave to go, I shall take it."

The C.O. said he would refer to the War Office. The answer came through that it would be all right for Starr to visit his home before returning to make the detailed report.

Starr took the train to Staffordshire, and a few hours later he was back with Michelle.

After the short leave which he had been given and which seemed all too brief, he returned to Guildford to complete the report. It was certainly a long job, and, still dying to be at home, the days dragged terribly while he was doing it. In it he put the whole story which appears

in this book, adding, when talking about the radio sections operated by the Germans, that it was his impression
that men had continued to be sent from London solely
in order to keep the Germans occupied while something
more important was going on, and that some, if not all,
of those sent straight into the hands of the Sicherheits
Dienst had been sent knowingly, to keep the game going
— that is, to make the Germans believe that the French
Section still had confidence that it was their own men
who were transmitting to them. If this were not so, he
could not understand how London could have carried
on, with all the warnings they had received. This, of
course, was only his impression, and perhaps he made a
mistake in writing it in his report.

One day after this he was told to report to an office in
London, where he was asked a few questions touching
minor points in his report, but no reference was made
to his summing up.

That day, while he was in London, he visited the little
club just off Piccadilly Circus where, before he went to
France, he used to meet members of the French Section.
Just as he was approaching this place, he encountered the
Newton brothers, whom he had met first at Wanborough
Manor, who had been put under his wing while training,
and with whom he had been able to exchange just a few
words at the Avenue Foch when they were brought in
for interrogation. They were very happy to see each
other and to learn that they were all still alive. The two
brothers had been in Buchenwald.

"What was going on at the Avenue Foch?" they asked him presently.

He explained briefly why he was there in the conditions of which they had glimpsed something.

"When we got back we were told that none of us was to speak to you if we met you," they said.

"Why not?"

"We don't know exactly. But in any case your word is good enough for us."

Although this seemed to him a bit strange, he thought perhaps the order (he thinks they referred to it as an order) had been given before his report had been completed, and that possibly conversation had been discouraged in order to prevent the unconscious confusion of accounts. It must be remembered that although he was managing to keep going and to do the things that were necessary as they presented themselves, he had only recently returned from overwhelming experiences, and was still in very much of a daze. In fact, for some time after his return he was not as sharp as he might have been normally.

One of the brothers said that they had been told, while in Buchenwald, that he had been down to the southwest of France with the Gestapo.

"Not me. One of the other boys," he said.

They seemed particularly surprised.

The three of them spent an hour or two together and he returned to Guildford. Here another longish time elapsed before he was instructed to report once more to the War Office, where he was told that his report was satisfactory and that he could go home on unlimited leave.

Before leaving for home he called in to see Miss Atkins (he cannot remember for what purpose, perhaps just to have a chat with her). As he entered her office he saw "Henri," the lieutenant who had introduced him to "Martin." "Henri" jumped up immediately when he saw Starr and said, "We got 'Martin'! We got him!"

Starr just nodded and greeted Miss Atkins. They talked for a few moments and then he turned to speak to "Henri," but found he had disappeared. He chatted a little more with Miss Atkins, and she smiled and said, "There were some quite amusing things in your report!" This was the only comment she ever made to him about it.

After this he left for home.

Some time later, during a trip to London, he had tea with Colonel Buckmaster and his wife at their flat. During the visit he said, "D'you know, I was rather disappointed when I got back to England."

"Why?"

"Well, I had expected at least to see you, on arrival, or some members of the French Section, and that there'd be some sort of a get-together. Instead of which, I was taken to Guildford without seeing anyone."

"Oh, well," Buckmaster said. "You see, when you came back everything was finished, and the section was disbanded."

Apart from this he cannot remember anything of the conversation, which must have gone no further than generalities. This, apart from being with the two brothers, was the last of his association with the French Section.

After this he went up to Staffordshire again, for he and the Newtons had decided to open a club together in Hanley.

He had been home for some while when he received a letter from the Judge Advocate General's office, saying that various members of the Avenue Foch Sicherheits Dienst were on trial, and Kieffer had asked whether Starr might go as a witness. He traveled immediately to Wuppertal, where the trial had already begun, and gave evidence for the defense. This was in March 1947.

Speaking under oath, he said, in answer to questions, that he had not been ill-treated at the Avenue Foch and had never known Kieffer to ill-treat any of his prisoners. He mentioned Kieffer's having brought biscuits and cigarettes to each of the cells on Sunday mornings, and said that to the best of his knowledge none of the members of S.O.E. French Section had been tortured at the Avenue Foch.

The president of the court asked him whether he could say that he saw *all* the prisoners. To this he had to answer, "No."

After he had given his evidence he was able to stay until the end of the proceedings. Kieffer was accused of having passed on an order for the shooting of six uniformed commandos captured at the time of the Nor-

mandy landings. These men had kept a rendezvous arranged by one of the German-controlled wireless sets
under the impression that they were going to join a genuine S.O.E. group, and of course were met by the Germans instead. Some of their comrades were there to give
evidence for the prosecution.

A verdict of "Guilty" was brought in, and a sentence
of death by hanging pronounced. Starr saw Kieffer's face
as he heard this, and was sure that the expression on it was
of amazement. Before he left the court he made a bow to
Starr. It was as if he had said, "You did what you could
for me."

In the mess afterwards one of the officers of the court
who had been sitting next to the prosecutor told Starr
that the prosecutor had expressed the very greatest astonishment at the sentence. The execution was carried out
very quickly.

For about two years Starr had still been on full Army
pay, since he could not be discharged until his health was
certified as recovered. Although he never at any point
broke up, he was certainly very much weakened, and for
quite a long time was in a rather critical condition. Michelle said that when he first came back he used to eat his
food crouched over his plate and with such concentration that it made her feel ill. One or two things like this
brought home to her what he had been through and the
conditions under which he had been living. Now, however, after a final medical, he was certified permanently
unfit for military service, and discharged from the Army

with the honorary rank of captain and a pension in respect of the gunshot wounds acquired at Dijon in 1943.

He had been interested in getting the club in Hanley organized, but now that it had got going he found the running of it and the type of life not very interesting. The brothers could carry on with it alone, and he decided to return to art and to his old job in Paris. So, with Michelle and their children, he returned to the flat at Issy-les-Moulineaux, and they took up life again where they had left it in 1939.

Some time after he had been in France he met, on the Champs Elysées, Claude Dauphin, the French film actor, with whom he had traveled from the South of France to Gibraltar after his first mission. Dauphin stared at him as though he had seen a ghost. "I asked Colonel Buckmaster what had become of you," he explained, "and he told me you were dead. He said you had been shot while in the field."

BOOK TWO

What Happened Afterwards

I

"A Borderline Case"

ON JUNE 16, 1949, I wrote to Colonel Maurice Buckmaster. I had found his name, for the first time, in a newspaper report containing the announcement of the award of the George Cross to my friend Noor Inayat Khan, alias "Madeleine." I was then planning to write the story of her life, and thought that he could give me some of the service details. Not knowing his address, I sent the letter care of the War Office, and some days later received a phone call. It was Colonel Buckmaster. He told me that he was just going out of England, but that he would give me the address of somebody who could tell me as much as he could, Miss Vera Atkins.[1]

I wrote to her, and subsequently went to see her. She hastened to assure me that although Noor had refused to give any information during her long interrogations at the Avenue Foch, she had not been tortured. She gave me the addresses of one or two people in England with whom Noor had trained, and of a person in Paris whom she described as "a French patriot" (whom I called X in my book, *Madeleine*).

Then she said, "There's another man I can give you,

[1] Squadron Officer, W.A.A.F.

who is rather an important witness in the story of
'Madeleine.'" She hesitated, and said carefully, considering her words, "He's not actually a traitor, but — he
tried to play a game with the Gestapo, and as that kind
of thing is never successful the result was that they
learned things from him."

She said that he was an Englishman, but was no longer
connected with the section. "We didn't take any action;
but he's gone to live in France now, and he isn't any
longer part of us in any way. We feel he let the side
down. And he was the only one who did. You can say
that he's a borderline case, really."

She told me that while a prisoner in the Avenue Foch
he had obtained considerable liberty of movement, the
Germans letting him walk about all over the place. Owing to this he, "Madeleine" and another prisoner had
managed to escape and had climbed out onto the roofs,
but had unfortunately been recaptured.

She did not see why he should not tell me the story of
this attempted escape and give me the details he could
remember. She said, "*I think* he would do that. He
could tell *that* story without blushing. Only you had
better make it clear that it is 'Madeleine' you want to
know about. Because if he thinks you are trying to pick
into his story he'll shut up at once, and you'll find him
very cagy. I should make it clear in your first letter that
you are writing a book about 'Madeleine,' and that it is
because he knew her that you want to see him." Otherwise, she thought, he might not answer it. "And when

you do get to see him, if you do, remember the sort of man you are dealing with. People who have done things like this get a certain sort of mentality. You may find that he's twisted things round in his mind by this time, and worked them into some kind of a peculiar story in which he is perfectly justified and the section seems to have done everything wrong."

I gathered that he must be a bit of a case.

She said, "You understand what a terrific inferiority complex can do! You'll probably find him very touchy and you'll have to use a great deal of tact. And, of course, you won't believe everything he says if he starts spinning some fantastic story."

Among the addresses with which she very helpfully supplied me there was one that she could not remember, and she said she would let me have it when we met next time. I got muddled with so many names, and thought, wrongly, that the peculiar Englishman's address was among those she had been able to give me. That evening, accordingly, I wrote what I hoped was a very tactful letter, mentioning the screwdriver he had lent to "Madeleine," but addressed it to X — a mistake that was to have interesting repercussions.

When I next saw Miss Atkins she said, "I still haven't been able to find Starr's address, but I can give you his brother's, and you can write and ask him for it." Accordingly, she gave me the address of Lieutenant Colonel George Starr, D.S.O., M.C., etc., in Brussels, who was "quite all right," remarking it was hard lines on him that his brother had got himself into disgrace. She gave me again all the same warnings about Starr, and I realized, but did not confess, that the person to whom I had sent the "tactful" letter was "the French patriot."

So that evening I wrote to "the French patriot," explaining that my first letter had been written under the impression that he was somebody else, and also to Colonel George Starr, asking him for the address of his brother, and explaining that I was writing a book about "Madeleine" and thought Captain John Starr might be able to tell me something about her detention at the Avenue Foch.

In due course I received a letter from George Starr saying he was sure his brother would be glad to give me all the help he was able, and enclosing his address.

I then wrote to John.

Very speedily I had a reply saying, "I can and will with pleasure give you considerable information about 'Madeleine' and our 'stay' at the Avenue Foch."

From "the French patriot" I had no reply.

2

On the fourteenth of September I met John Starr at his home in Issy-les-Moulineaux. I must say that I arrived wondering what I was going to meet and prepared to conduct a very "tactful" interview. The door was opened by a shortish man, rather gentle in manner, who brought me in, introduced me to his wife and asked me to sit down on the sofa. He sat beside me and said, "I'll have to tell you some of my story first, because otherwise you won't understand how the parts about your friend fit in."

Madame Starr brought in some tea and stayed for a while having it with us. He started his story from the point of his arrest in Dijon, after he had been parachuted into the Juras, and carried on through his transfer to Fresnes and to the Avenue Foch. With Miss Atkins's warnings in mind, I must say that when he described how he had copied out a big map for the Germans I wondered if this was not a euphemistic way of saying he had made one, and similarly when he told me about the documents he had copied. He gave me that evening practically all the details which figure in the relevant chapter of *Madeleine*, and some that I did not put in, continuing his own story a little beyond that point. He explained the dilemma in which Kieffer had placed him when he asked him for his word of honor not to attempt to escape again, and the choice he had made. "I thought I'd find a way of getting the information out somehow. But it just didn't come off."

I realized that he had given me a great deal of material about "Madeleine," and was grateful to him for it. Besides, his story had a genuine ring, to which, almost despite myself, I warmed, although I had received such a warning that I felt that I ought to accept it with some reserve. I had the impression that I was listening to an account of something that had really happened, yet kept pulling myself up, asking myself whether I was not being deceived by a very plausible interpretation of a history that was not, perhaps, so straightforward as it sounded.

When he had come to an end — which was quite late in the evening — I asked, "Is all this for publication?"

He seemed surprised by the question, and said, "Yes. Except that perhaps you'd better not put in about the Germans operating the radio sets and meeting our boys on the field. They might not like it in London."

"I can put in that you say you were copying a map and documents?"

"Of course. It's a rather necessary part of the story, isn't it?"

He walked with me to the Métro, and all the way I was wondering what to think about him. What I had been told in London weighed very heavily on me; yet I found myself saying, "I think I know the truth when I hear it."

As we were about to say good-by, he added, "If there's anything else you think of that you want to know, you can write and ask me."

Then he said with a slight hesitation that I noticed, "Well — give my regards to Miss Atkins — if you think that would be appreciated."

I hesitated in my turn and said, "I'm not quite sure."

"Oh well, then, don't bother."

3

This interview left me perplexed and, more than that, troubled. The question of Starr had got under my skin. I thought a lot about it and him, and wondered if there had not been some mistake somewhere.

When I saw Miss Atkins I told her the impression I had of him was sympathetic rather than otherwise. I felt she was annoyed. She asked me what he had told me, and I repeated the whole story, except that instead of saying that the information he had wanted to get back to London was that the Germans were working the radio sets, I just said "about things he had learned." Although still green in these matters, I felt that the part about the radio sets was dangerous.

"Oh, that's probably true as far as it goes," she replied. "It may very well have been quite genuine in the beginning. I'm willing to believe that he had the intention, in the beginning, to get information back to us. Only afterwards, after they had tried to get away and been recaptured and he knew he couldn't do it, then there wasn't any longer any justification for his continuing to enjoy privileges not allowed to any other prisoner. He should have said, 'This has got to come to an end now,' and *insisted* on being put back in a prison and being kept like the others."

She compared him with "Madeleine" and Faye, very much to his detriment, saying that they had chosen the hard road, which led to the concentration camp, in refusing to give an undertaking not to escape again. "I'm convinced that, when it came to it, Starr found he just couldn't face being sent to a concentration camp. He was sent to one in the end, but he put it off as long as possible, temporizing in one way and another. And later on he got into a position in which he absolutely blotted his copybook. There could be no justification whatever for some of the things that happened." And after a moment she added, "He always used to be so cocksure of himself. He never thought that could happen to him."

Then she remarked, "I suppose he spoke very unpleasantly about us?"

"No. As a matter of fact, he didn't. He didn't say anything about personalities. But he did say there had been mistakes made in the section. He didn't say it unpleasantly. He" — I took my courage in both my hands — "he said the Germans were operating some of the radio sets, belonging to our operators whom they had captured, back to London."

"Oh yes; that did happen with some of them. Was that all he said?"

"Yes."

It seemed to me she had been expecting something else, and I was puzzled.

A short while afterwards she told me that Colonel Buckmaster was back in London and asked me if I would like to see him. I said, "Of course," and she gave me his phone number. I telephoned him and we arranged a meeting. So it was that I met him for the first and only time. He asked me whom I had seen already for information about "Madeleine," and I mentioned Starr. As the question of his *bona fides* was still very much on my mind, I asked (the words still cause me to blush), "What d'you think of Starr?"

He replied, with considerable force, "Nothing! After he'd been taken by the Gestapo he did everything they asked him for a year!"

Rather flattened out by this, I was silent.

"Well, almost everything," he said more moderately.

He asked me what Starr had told me, so I repeated the story once more, though I did not mention the radio sets this time. At one point he said, "Well, that's probably true, as far as it goes."

"He says quite definitely that he didn't give them any information."

"That may be true, in a sense. I don't know that he'd any in particular to give."

He asked me to go on. When I came to the point where Starr obtained the screwdriver by means of which the escape from the Avenue Foch was made possible, and mentioned that he passed it on to "Madeleine" and Faye, he interrupted me, "But in that case, if he was organizing everything and got them the things, one rather wonders why he didn't go with them."

"But he did!" I exclaimed.

"You've only got his word for that. And that's worth nothing!" After a moment he added, "I never trusted the man. I never trusted him even from the beginning."

Later I asked him whether he wanted to read *Madeleine* when it was finished, before it was published.

He said he did not think that was necessary, but suggested that I had better show Starr anything that I was writing about him, as otherwise he might sue me for libel.

"I shall show it to him. But I can't see how he could sue me for libel considering it's exactly what he told me himself."

"All the same, he may not like it when he sees it in print. You'd better send him a copy, and then you'll be covered. A man like that, with a terrific inferiority complex, wouldn't hesitate to bring an action for defamation if he thought he'd been damaged."

4

In November, to my great surprise, I received a much-belated reply from "the French patriot," inviting me to lunch. This was really most annoying, because I was now back in London. However, as he was an important witness, I felt I had to go.

"Madeleine's" brother, Vilayat Inayat Khan, had just come to England, and suggested that I should stay in the family house in Suresnes, the suburb of Paris where they had all grown up, and gave me a note to a doctor and his wife who lived on the top floor, authorizing them to let me in and give me a room and — most important — access to his papers. This was because I had many times asked him for a certain document regarding his sister, which he either forgot or could not find. As he was not sure in which file he had put it he could only suggest I should go through all I could see.

I arrived in the evening and was let in by the young doctor. He showed me into a room littered with blood-stained handkerchiefs and rags — rather startling until I remembered that Vilayat had had his arm in a sling when I saw him in London, as a result of a collision with a moving vehicle on the Place de la Concorde — "*la chambre de Vilayat.*" Next we went into the kitchen, which was in a state of indescribable confusion, with pots and pans all over the place — "*la cuisine de Vilayat*" — and finally into the sitting room, where something was the matter with the light, so that we had to grope our way in with a torch to a desk piled high with a pyramid of papers — "*le bureau de Vilayat.*"

I decided to leave the search for the document until the daytime.

My luncheon appointment with X, as I shall now call "the French patriot," was for twelve o'clock. I arrived punctually, had some time to wait as he had gone out, and then, when he and his wife did arrive, shortly to be followed by another gentleman who I learned was a lawyer, I was offered Martinis, one after another, with nothing to eat, until nearly two o'clock. When I tried occasionally to mention the subject of "Madeleine," he dismissed it, almost as though it were bad form, saying, "Business after lunch!"

In the end my head was violently aching from all the drinks I had been given, and I said I would not have another before having anything to eat. That did the trick, and the lunch was produced, a very lavish one indeed — like his whole apartment.[1] After that — it took some time — we were brought back into the drawing room for coffee and liqueurs. By this time I had such a headache, and was so bored and fed up, that I took very little part in the conversation that was going on. At length I hinted once more that I should like to work.

X got up, motioned to the lawyer, and the three of us went into another room, which was an office. There we sat down at a table, the atmosphere became quite different, and X said, "I've made one statement to the police already. Why have you come to see me?"

Considerably surprised, I replied, "I shouldn't have thought of going to the police to ask anything you could tell me."

The lawyer said to him soothingly, "Miss Fuller is a writer. She comes to get local color."

He allowed himself to be somewhat reassured, but not, I felt, altogether. He asked, "Who did you think I was when you wrote me the first letter?"

I apologized for the mistake, and said I had muddled him up with somebody who had been a prisoner at the Avenue Foch at the same as "Madeleine," and who had

---

[1] I was told afterwards that he was a business magnate or financier and enormously wealthy, which his address and the apartment certainly suggested.

lent her a screwdriver with the aid of which they had tried to escape.

He seemed very interested in this story, and asked more questions about this person he had been taken for. "I think I've seen him. A short man, with a small mustache and a face like a moon?"

"I suppose you could describe him like that."

"What was his name?"

"Starr."

I knew the moment I had said this that I had made a mistake. But it was too late to take it back.

"I didn't know the name before," he said thickly. "What's his address?"

"I haven't got it with me." (I could remember it, but I was not going to give it away.)

"He was in the pay of the Gestapo."

My heart sank — and for several reasons. I felt I had a loyalty to Starr, who I was sure had given me all he could about "Madeleine." I had an absolute obligation not to let him suffer for having done that, and I could have kicked myself for having let his name slip.

"He used to write things in on a map," said X. "I could see him doing it, while I was being interrogated myself, in the mirror behind the interrogator's head."

When at last he got down to telling me of his connection with "Madeleine," the lawyer took notes, which struck me as peculiar. The story which X told me was full of what I knew to be misstatements, and after a little time I realized that it was a case, not of making mistakes, but of lying. I wondered for what reason. He accused three more people of treachery and other unpleasant things in what seemed to me a most irresponsible manner. I came away with an impression of real badness such as I had rarely met in my life, and very much shaken.

Before we parted he had told me that a Frenchwoman was going to be tried in ten days' time for having given "Madeleine" to the Gestapo. That startling piece of intelligence was the one concrete thing I had obtained. I could not, however, stay until the trial, and would have to tell Vilayat when I got back to London the next day, so as to give him the chance of being there.

It was dark when I returned to the house in Suresnes, and so, in the big, dim, disordered sitting room, I had to continue my search for the document in the feeble circle of light that could be shone on just one spot at a time.

It was, I believe, nearly two in the morning when I came upon a document which was not the one I was looking for, but something like it. I began reading with increasing interest. It was from a Mr. Denis McFarlin, who had spoken with a German woman in Pforzheim, where "Madeleine" had been sent after the escape from the Avenue Foch, and it told, briefly, the story of the escape, as it had been told by "Madeleine" to that German woman in 1944. It mentioned that she went with two male officers across the roofs, and that they had been picked out by the searchlights when there was a raid.

Although I believed Starr, I had been worried by Buckmaster's saying that there was no proof that he went with the other two; and it seemed like "Madeleine" speaking from the dead.

It occurred to me that very probably Starr had no documentary evidence at all, and that this, slender as it was, would at least be something. Haunted by the feeling that X was plotting against him, I detached it from the file and put it in my bag.

I traveled back to England the next day and wrote immediately to Starr — half wondering whether it was really my business to warn somebody who was supposed to be either a traitor or the next thing to it — telling him that I had inadvertently given his name to someone who I feared had unfriendly intentions towards him, and also that I had found a document which confirmed the story of the triple escape which he had told me. I wondered if he would be offended by my saying this, as though it needed proof; but decided that as he must have had a good deal of trouble in London he probably would not. He wrote back, thanking me for my letter, and saying that while always aware that the story was true, he was glad that I had found confirmation of it.

On the following day I saw Vilayat, told him of my interview with X and of the forthcoming trial and gave him Starr's address, in return for a promise not to disclose it to anybody else. He then went back to Paris to learn what he could on his own account.

On the night following the trial, Vilayat, now back in

London, came to see me. He was in a terrible rage, partly because of the verdict and partly on account of something he had learned about X. He had seen X shortly before the trial. After telling him gratuitously that he was having Starr investigated, X had spun him a long story, about as unsatisfactory — though not the same — as the one he had told me, culminating in an allegation that "Madeleine" had given a friend of his a rendezvous with the Gestapo at the Porte de Levallois. When Vilayat demanded to know the name of this friend, X said he did not know.

"You dare to tell me my sister betrayed a friend of yours, and then say you don't know his name!"

X had seemed to become frightened, and had murmured, "Viennot."

"And his address?"

Again X had replied that he did not know, but under pressure he had gone back on his first statement and said that Viennot was not his friend, but his lawyer's.

Vilayat had telephoned immediately to the lawyer before X had time to do so, asking for Viennot's address and not explaining the reason. The lawyer had given it to him.

Vilayat had gone at once to see Viennot, who lived in the Quartier Latin, and who received him in a perfectly simple and direct manner. He said that he had worked with "Madeleine" in the field, but denied absolutely that she had betrayed him. All he knew about the Porte de Levallois was that once she had asked him to meet her there and had not come herself. He spoke of her with regard and affection.

Then Viennot had told Vilayat his version of the story, which was a very different one from X's. X, he said, had been captured by the Germans, and while a prisoner had given "Madeleine" a rendezvous with the Gestapo on the Avenue MacMahon, which Viennot, scenting danger, had not allowed her to keep. He had gone out in a car himself, to see how the land lay, and had driven through the ambush, which to his experienced eye was completely transparent. This had taken place about a fortnight before "Madeleine's" arrest following, apparently, an independent denunciation.

I was surprised that X should have been such a fool as to give Vilayat the name of so fatal a witness against himself. However, I knew that Vilayat could look rather terrifying when he was angry — his dark Indian eyes helped — and I could only suppose that X had been shaken into such a jelly that he had temporarily lost control of his wits.

On the evening before the trial Vilayat had seen Starr, who he said had received him perfectly nicely and told him what he could remember of his sister. The great thing for Vilayat was to have his assurance that she had not been tortured at the Avenue Foch.

At the court the next day he had been startled to find X the solitary witness for the defense. The woman on trial, whom he now saw for the first time, was accused of having sold Noor Inayat Khan, alias "Madeleine," to the Sicherheits Dienst for a hundred thousand francs (about a hundred pounds). Vilayat himself had given evidence for the prosecution; but the only witness of substance for the prosecution had been Ernest. Ernest, whom he saw also for the first time, and who was himself still a prisoner of the French, told the court how he had made the arrest of "Madeleine." For Vilayat, who heard the details for the first time, it was naturally exceedingly painful.

During the hearing Starr had suddenly appeared in the court and had come up to Vilayat, saying, "I'm very sorry to trouble you while you're in the middle of all this, but I'd be very grateful if you could spare me a few minutes. I've just been charged with 'intelligence with the enemy.' "

Vilayat followed him out into a foyer, where a French officer was waiting, a Captain Mercier. Mercier explained that he had asked Starr if he could produce any evidence in support of his escape from the Avenue Foch, and that Starr had shown him my letter saying that I had found such a document in Vilayat's file. As I had said also that I had taken the document to England, Mercier asked Vilayat if he remembered it and would sign a statement that he possessed it, which Vilayat, with a rather hazy memory of what he had in his file, agreed to do. I now showed him the letter at his request, and he heaved a sigh of relief.

After the conversation with Mercier he had gone back into court. Then it had seemed to him like the last straw when the counsel for the defense produced a letter written in 1945 by Colonel Buckmaster to the woman on trial, thanking her for her services and the assistance she had rendered to the members of his organization. "Which are you going to believe?" counsel cried, waving the letter in the air. "This Gestapo man, or the English Colonel Buckmaster?"

The woman was acquitted by the panel of nine military judges by five votes to four. After it was over, Vilayat asked permission to speak to Ernest, but this was not allowed.

Still very angry and upset, he now suggested that we should try to see Miss Atkins. It was about nine o'clock in the evening. Using my phone, we rang her; she was in, and said we could come over straight away.

At her flat Vilayat told his whole story over again. Very bitterly he mentioned that it was not only his sister who had lost her life as the result of her denunciation. "Of course you know that her radio set was afterwards operated by the Germans for months."

She nodded almost imperceptibly.

We talked until late, and important and peculiar matters relating to the case which had just been tried were revealed.[1] At one moment Miss Atkins spoke of Kieffer, and said that she had met him in January 1947, the year of his trial. I was struck by her remark that at

[1] After considerable reflection, I decided that to enter at all adequately into the discussion of the very odd facts relating to this case (of which I was to hear more later in other quarters) would extend the scope of this narrative so much as to be irrelevant in this book.

that time there had been nothing against him, as the affair of the commandos shot in Normandy had not then been raised. "If that had not come up he would still be walking about today," she said. "They had nothing else against him." She also said that Goetz, whom she had met, was not at all a typical Gestapo man, but much superior, and she imagined that it was the same with Ernest, whom she had not met. She thought that those two were the best minds in the Avenue Foch.

Vilayat, who was still feeling very sore, told the story of the Avenue MacMahon and X; but Miss Atkins said nothing. Later she spoke of X with sympathy, saying that although his statements might not always be satisfactory she thought it was because his memory was defective. The generosity which she displayed towards X surprised me in its contrast with her attitude to Starr.

We spoke of Starr again during this evening, and I remarked that if the messages which he had buried in the flower pots on the roofs off the Avenue Foch could be dug up they should help his case very much. She made a bit of a face and said, "Well, they're his flower pots! It's for him to go and look for them if he wants to justify himself. But he'd better take a witness, or people will think he's just put them there now!"

I said I was going to write to him suggesting that he should go back to the Avenue Foch with witnesses, perhaps Mercier and myself, to try to find those flower pots, because if the messages had not decayed completely they would constitute absolute proof of his attempted escape.

She said shortly, "That doesn't need proving. We know that's true. We've always known it."

I was glad to hear this, but surprised, as Colonel Buckmaster had told me the contrary.

"If that escape had been successful," she conceded, "and Starr had been able to bring back to London, from the H.Q. of the Gestapo, all the information he had collected, he would have been one of the great heroes of the war. There would probably have been a book about him! But it just didn't happen that way. After they were recaptured, he found he couldn't face being sent to concentration camp, as the others were. He didn't want to give up the privileges he had got used to at the Avenue Foch, although, after he had given his word of honor not to escape again, there was no longer any justification for his retaining them. Instead of saying, 'Well, I had a shot, but now the game's up!' and *insisting* on being kept under normal conditions of detention, he allowed himself to be put in a position that was quite indefensible. He must have known that he was a most demoralizing spectacle for every other prisoner that was brought in. He couldn't even have *thought* that it was something that could be justified. We consider that he absolutely blotted his copybook."

II

Tribunal Militaire

I EXCHANGED A COUPLE of letters with Starr after this, mainly about the text of the Avenue Foch chapter of *Madeleine* which I had sent him. Then on the thirtieth of December I went again to Paris for further research for the book. New Year's Eve is a great festival for the French and I had difficulty in finding a hotel. At last, in desperation, I rang Starr to see if he could help, and he said he would book a room in a small hotel near their flat, and would pick me up and take me out there.

It was bitterly cold, and I was glad when his car drew up beside me.

"Vilayat tells me that you're in a spot of trouble," I said as I got in. Although it had been implicit, he had not mentioned in his letters that he had been charged.

"What?"

"With the French military."

"Oh, that!"

"What's going to happen now? Do you have to stand court martial?"

"I don't know. It depends on whether I can satisfy Captain Mercier."

"Can they, in fact, try a British officer by French court martial?"

"Yes."

"Have you ever been charged before?"

"No."

"Were you never charged in London?"

"No."

"Amazing!" I said this with great force, and only realized, in the moment's silence that followed, how strangely it sounded. Trying to retrieve it, I said, "I don't mean that I think you should have been. I only mean that considering the way they speak about you in London it is extraordinary to me that they didn't charge you."

He showed some interest now, although he did not immediately press for details. "Nobody's ever said anything officially to me in London," he remarked, "although, from one or two things I've learned in a roundabout fashion, I've had a suspicion that people must have been talking about me in a funny way."

"I can't understand it," I said. "I can't understand it at all. I feel as if you have been judged behind your back without being given a hearing."

"Exactly. If they thought I'd done something wrong, why didn't they say so to me? From what you say, they must think I'm — a traitor." There was just a slight hesitation, as though it was the first time he had pronounced the word. "In that case, they should have charged me. I would much rather have had a court martial than this sort of thing."

"Perhaps they weren't sure," I said. "Not sure enough to bring a charge."

He exploded. "If you think that a man *may* be a traitor, but you're not *sure*, you *find out!* Why didn't they tackle me while I was in Guildford or London? They could have asked me about anything they didn't find satisfactory. Here," he said, "a French soldier came to the door, rang the bell, and put an envelope into my hands with a paper inside it saying, *You are charged with intelligence with the enemy.* I like it better that way. I know where I am."

He began to tell me about the proceedings, and his sense of humor asserted itself as he warmed up to the account. To start with, when he had gone down to the Tribunal and presented himself as he had been summoned to do, Mercier had addressed him as "Monsieur Starr." He had replied, "Captain Starr, Captain Mercier!"

"But wasn't it a wartime rank?"

"No. It is an honorary rank which was conferred on me for life, after the war, when I was discharged. Only the King can take it away from me. I could go round calling myself Captain Starr if I liked, though I generally don't."

After that, he resumed, he had taken out a packet of cigarettes and offered Mercier one. The latter had refused it, saying, "You're here to answer a charge."

Next Mercier had told him that he had the right to obtain legal advice before answering any questions.

Starr had said he didn't want any.

"But it is your right. You can go away now and consult your lawyer, and come back when he has advised you on the best way to present your case."

"I don't need any advice of that sort. I have a plain story to tell, and I'm willing to answer straight away any questions you have the right to ask me."

Mercier had thawed somewhat to this answer and had said, "Very well, if that's the way you want it, you'd better tell me your whole story from the beginning. Take your time, and include everything."

He had done so. Towards the end of the interview there was quite a different atmosphere.

"So what happens now?" I asked.

"I don't know. He said he'd have to check up on all the things I'd told him, as far as it was possible, and I imagine that'll take some time."

Since this interview Mercier had already seen Commert, one of Starr's former cellmates in Fresnes, and had phoned Starr to tell him that Commert confirmed his account of the conversations they had had when Starr was considering whether he should agree to do the copying at the Avenue Foch. He thought it was nice of Mercier to have phoned to tell him that the checkup had supported his statement.

One point had arisen at the interview not strictly concerning his case. Starr had mentioned that he was betrayed by one "Martin," and that he had been told by "Henri" after the war that this "Martin" was dead. Mercier had said he would like to ask "Henri" for details, as he was interested in tracing "Martin," and if he was dead would like to know it. He had asked Starr, therefore, if he could give him the real name of "Henri." Starr was not sure whether it was in order, even now, to give the real names corresponding to code names, and said he would have to ask our people. After leaving Mercier, he had gone to the British consulate, had explained the circumstances, and asked them to forward this question to our people in London. He had been told to call in after some days for a reply. When he did so, he was told that the reply which had come was: "Leave the country immediately." There was no answer to the question about "Henri."

I did not get the whole significance at first — or for some time. When I did, I was shocked and revolted.

"If I were to leave the country now," he said, "with a thing like this pending, I should never be able to show my face again either here or anywhere else in the world. It's not for *my* sake that they sent the message," he went on. "Once an inquiry starts, nobody knows where it will end. There have been mistakes made in the section that they wouldn't like to come out in court if I had to reveal them in my defense." After a pause, he added with something like a sigh, yet grimly, "It just means I shall have to bat in on my own, saying as little as I can."

Perhaps because I was a soldier's daughter, I was deeply angry at the advice he had been given — to run, when a charge had been made against him. This did more than any other single thing to bring about a revulsion in my feeling towards London.

"What's one man?" he said, a trifle sadly. "In a thing like this, one man matters very little."

I recollected that I had a confession to make. "I'm afraid it's I who got you into all this!" And I told him how I had come to give his name to the man X, who had, evidently, asked at the Tribunal for him to be investigated. "I'm so sorry."

"That's all right, Miss Fuller," he said in a voice that was full of a very genuine kindness. "It may all be for the best, in the end."

I felt that only a good man would have said that.

We had reached the hotel where he had booked a room for me. "Is it too late for you to come back to our place and work tonight?" he asked. "Michelle will make some tea and something to eat, and we could go through that typescript and I'll draw those roofs for you."

I took my case up and deposited it in my room, and then rejoined him in the car.

"What d'you think yourself?" he asked. "Tell me honestly. Do you think I'm a traitor?"

"No," I said.

Michelle received me with a smile and brought in tea and sandwiches. We began to work immediately. Starr produced the typescript of the Avenue Foch chapters of

Madeleine which I had sent him and went through them with me, correcting a few mistakes. Then he drew me, from memory, a plan and some sketches of the roofs of 84 Avenue Foch and the adjoining houses, such as could only have been made by someone who had been on top of them. He agreed that on the following Tuesday, when he was taking me to the Tribunal to see Mercier, to whom I was going to hand the original letter I had taken from Vilayat's file, we should ask Mercier to come to the Avenue Foch and he would take us both up and show us the roofs. But he had not much hope, after seven and a half years, of finding the notes he had buried in the flower pots. "They were on tissue paper, and they'll have moldered long ago. I spoke of them in my report and they ought to have been looked for by the French Section." The great thing, he thought, was to show that the roofs corresponded with the drawings he had been able to make beforehand.

"About this man X who wants to pin something on me," he asked. "What did he say to you?"

"He said you were in the pay of the Gestapo."

"In that case, they *had* to investigate," he said quietly. I realized he was glad to learn that the French military were not busying themselves with a purely frivolous inquiry, and that he should have had such a reaction, at such a moment, showed me how much he loved France. "If that's what he told *them*," he said, "it was their duty to make inquiries."

"He says that while he was being interrogated he

could see you, in the mirror behind the interrogator's head, drawing things on a map."

"He could have seen me drawing on the map, but only in a normal way — I mean, by coming into the room where I was working, which was the guardroom, where in fact prisoners were often brought in to wait. He couldn't possibly have seen it in the mirror behind Ernest's head — there *was* one — because Ernest's room and the guardroom were side by side and there was a solid wall in between them. I suppose it was more interesting to see it in a mirror!"

I wondered whether I should tell him all I knew about X, but decided to wait until I had seen Viennot and heard from his own lips about the incident on the Avenue MacMahon.

He asked, "Have you spoken about me with Colonel Buckmaster?"

"Yes."

"What did he say?"

"He said that after you had been captured by the Gestapo you did everything, or almost everything, they asked you for a year."

The reaction did not come with as much violence as I had expected. He looked at me very straight for some moments, with incredibly wide eyes, saying nothing. Then he said, "It's about what I expected. I had the feeling that he was saying something of the sort about me, though I didn't know."

As I found several times with Starr, the explosion

came a minute or two later. It was a case of delayed re-action. We had gone on talking when he exclaimed suddenly, with great emotion, "I never did anything for them!"

He got up and went to fetch Michelle, who had gone into another room.

When she came back he said, "Miss Fuller has just told me Buckmaster said to her that after I'd been captured I did everything they asked me for a year."

Michelle was naturally very distressed. We talked about it and he said, "If he really believed that, he should have had me charged — it was his duty."

As we went on discussing the situation which had been revealed he said, "I ask you! A perfectly genuine colonel thinks that one of the men whom he sent out turned traitor and worked for the Germans for a year. So he has him to tea with his wife and himself, talks pleasantly, asks him what he thinks of doing now the war is over, shakes hands with him and says good-by. Does that make sense?"

What impressed me most during this evening was his complete openness in all our discussions of the situation. He did not take umbrage. I found that I could say or ask practically anything that was in my mind without causing offense. Nobody could have been easier to talk to. He never blinked an implication. I could see no sign of the touchiness I had been led to expect in London; he had as little of it as any human being in the world could have had. He was quiet-spoken, moderate in his choice of words, and sensible. I felt that no man could have acted better in an extremely testing situation. In short, I was most impressed. His whole character, as it came over to me, was one of honesty and decency.

"If this is really what they think, I shouldn't have to learn about it from someone who is outside the service," he said. "They should have talked to me straight. That's where I reproach them."

We talked until very late. Michelle wanted him to take some action. She was a quiet person, but I glimpsed a certain fire.

"There's nothing L can do," he said. "Not as things stand at present."

"But for the children . . ."

"If they don't know their own father, it's a poor look-out."

She looked very sad, and Starr said he would think about it.

He took me down in the lift, and as we settled in the car I suggested that it might be a good idea if he went to see Miss Atkins. "After the affair here is settled, of course."

He was against the idea at first, but after a bit he relented and said, "Yes; on second thoughts I think I would like to see her some day. It may be that Miss Atkins doesn't understand how things were there. Maybe if I had a talk with her I could make her see it. I'll think about it later, anyway."

He began telling me about the dinner which he had

had with some of Kieffer's men in the restaurant, and about the trip on which he had gone with them "to find a field for a Hudson."

This shook me afresh. It was the first time he had told me he had been out with them, and I felt my stomach sinking as I realized there had been more to his situation at the Avenue Foch than the copying he had told me of. I did not at once get the strategic point, and, very new to these things, the first fact that hit me was simply that he had been out with the Gestapo and taken them somewhere.

Collecting myself, I asked him to tell me that story all over again as I had not got it yet. He did so, and this time I understood the point he was making — that the impossible location should have warned London.

"But it was sailing fearfully near the wind," I said. "Didn't it worry you that it must have *looked* as if you were with them and that you'd have to explain it when you got home?"

"No. I never thought I'd be doubted by my own people. That's the truth.

"Well, what d'you think yourself?" he asked me, for the second time that night. "D'you think I'm a traitor?"

"No," I said. "I don't think you're a traitor."

So he left me at the door of my hotel, and I went up to my room, my head reeling from all I had learned. The situation which had come to my knowledge had shaken me profoundly. At the same time, if *I* were making a mistake, letting myself be led on by a man against whom I had been warned virtually by the War Office, as I understood it, I was without excuse. I felt very alone; and with these events still seething in my mind, lay down at last to spend an entirely sleepless night.

It was to be the first of a number this affair was to cost me.

2

Neither did the problem resolve itself with the daylight. It was deeply troubling. When I was with Starr I was convinced of his integrity. I never had any difficulty in talking with him, such as a lack of frankness on the other side usually gives me. Usually I have faith in my judgment of people. Yet with a question of treason in the air, I hardly felt that I had the right to vest my confidence in purely personal "feel." The authority of Miss Atkins and Buckmaster, as representing the War Office, was enormous, and I could not easily dismiss what they had said.

And yet I was coming to believe that Starr was right and they were wrong. I didn't like the business of "Leave the country immediately." Why did they want him to sacrifice his honor — a British officer? Wasn't it, in truth, because they were afraid he might talk to the French about the mistakes made in London? Above all, if there really was question of his loyalty, why had there not been a court martial in England — and the whole thing made public? They seemed to have been soft:

why? There was nobody on "our" side with whom I felt I could talk about it usefully: I had to use my own judgment. I believed I had stumbled across a serious matter; and if I was right, it was one that could be dealt with properly only at a high level.

The next three days I spent in seeing other people concerned in the history of "Madeleine," including Viennot. I learned that he had been the organizer of an autonomous Resistance group, unconnected, except by accident, with the French Section. He told me the story of the rendezvous which X had given "Madeleine" on the Avenue MacMahon, with all the details related in my book. The question arose how I was going to represent this. Was I to put in X's name?

"If it was me," said Madame Viennot, "I would."

"That's equivalent to denunciation," I said, and asked Viennot what he felt about it.

He said he would be prepared to make a full statement either at the Tribunal or at the War Office, but that unless asked to do so he did not feel it was incumbent on him to take the first step. The question of denunciation was always unpleasant.

"*He* doesn't think so," I said. And, without mentioning the name, I told him that X had just got somebody I knew investigated.

Viennot was quite pained, and, turning to his wife, he exclaimed, "What d'you think of that? X went and denounced somebody!"

I suggested that after we had written the whole thing

down we should send X a copy, asking whether he had any reason to advance why it should not be published. Madame Viennot nearly jumped out of her chair at this, and in the end I said I thought Viennot and I ought to go and see him together and face him with it. Viennot agreed willingly. He had not seen X since the incident on the Avenue MacMahon, but would try to arrange an interview. He did not seem to bear much malice, and indeed appeared to take it as almost normal, or at any rate very much to be expected, that when a man had been arrested he gave away his colleagues.

"It was silly of him to pretend he hadn't done it," said Madame Viennot. "Nobody wants to stick a pin in him!"

We talked for about four hours. Although not a "tough" himself, Viennot had run a group of which the muscle was chiefly composed of gangsters from the Paris underworld — jewel and fur thieves, traffickers in prohibited commodities, and so on, mostly accustomed to the use of the cosh or pistol in civil life. He told the most amazing stories, casually mentioning, just as something amusing, that in 1943 he had been lunching four or five days a week with German officials, including some from the Avenue Foch, sometimes finding lady friends for them (prostitutes whom he had groomed to pass as superior women and taught to act as spies).

When I asked him if he would mind my writing all this in *Madeleine* he said, "Of course not. Anything you like. I don't mind at all."

He had once spent a week end with Kieffer at a country house where they had been hunting together. He did not seem to bear Kieffer any malice either, and described him as "not disagreeable," though he had been very badly beaten by the Sicherheits Dienst (not at the Avenue Foch) when his clandestine activities had been discovered. After that he had spent a long period in Mauthausen.

As he told his story, touching here and there on human weakness, vice and betrayal, I realized that this was a world in which ethics and values were at once more complicated and more ingenuous, more a matter for private conscience, than in a society with more regularly framed rules. By the time I left Viennot's house, Starr's little bluff seemed as innocent as a child's.

Nine o'clock next morning, the day when we were to see Mercier, found me at Issy-les-Moulineaux, coming up in the lift. Starr opened the door, and almost as soon as I was inside his flat I said, "I met somebody yesterday who told me that the man who asked for you to be investigated gave 'Madeleine' a rendezvous with the Gestapo a fortnight before she was arrested."

This time his reaction was immediate. His eyes opened, then he dived into the kitchen to bring out Michelle, so that they could hear the story together.

He was really quite jubilant. To Michelle he said, "It's what I was saying the other evening. I'm sure it's the men who have done something wrong themselves who have said things against me — it's just the same here and in London. If *those* people were checked, they'd get all the real traitors!"

I asked him if he knew the name of the man who had asked for him to be investigated. He shook his head.

"It seems to me you're entitled to know," I said. "Shall I tell you?"

"Not unless you want to. It isn't material."

I realized that in a sense he did not want to be the recipient of tales.

"I think I will, all the same," I said. And I did.

"I don't know him," he said. "Well, I never did any harm to *him*, anyway."

I was impressed because he did not show vindictiveness. If he had done, it would have been so very excusable.

"This is really a most ironic situation," I said. "Because it's really he who ought to be denounced. Only I suppose we just aren't the sort of people to do it . . . ?"

He sighed, and said, "Let's go!"

After having phoned Mercier, who gave us an appointment for noon, he drove me to 84 Avenue Foch, to see the concierge and make sure that it would be possible for us to get in when we came back with Mercier.

As we were very much too early now for our appointment at the Tribunal, we stopped in the Champs Elysées and had coffee. "It's obvious," he said. "If a chap has done something wrong, what will he do when he gets back? Discredit the witness." And he told me a few stories, without names, of things he had seen and heard in the Avenue Foch.

We returned to the car, but as we were still too early for our appointment drove around a bit and pulled up on the Quai Saint Bernard. He told me about two more of his trips from the Avenue Foch, into the country looking for bridges and so on, and with Placke on the occasion when the latter ended up by having to lie to his chief.

"Did you gather from your conversations in London whether the Germans actually learned anything from me?" he asked, very seriously.

"I think so," I said. "On the first evening that we met, Miss Atkins said that you tried to play a game with the Gestapo and that the result was that they learned things from you."

"I'm sorry," he said, and was silent for some moments. "If that is so, I'm sorry. It wasn't intentional. I don't claim to be a wonder man. When one is under repeated interrogation over a very long period, and one has to remember what one has said on previous occasions, one can only do one's best. I don't think anyone can ever be quite sure he hasn't made a slip somewhere. Though I honestly don't know what it could have been. I've been going over in my mind, since the last time we met, all the things that happened, and I can't think what I could have given away. Did she say?"

"No."

"Did she say where it was? During the interrogations at Dijon or at the Avenue Foch?"

"At the Avenue Foch, I think, since she referred to your playing a game."

"I wish you'd ask her what it was. I should like to know," he said simply.

"I will do that."

After a moment I added that her quarrel with him seemed to be mainly concerned with his position after he had given his word of honor, and the impression it created. "She says you were a demoralizing spectacle."

"Which was the more demoralizing — to see me sitting there, or to find that the Germans were working the radio sets back to London and meeting our men on the field?"

He started up the car again. "You can't make an omelet without breaking a few eggs," he said as we crossed the bridge. "The trouble with my affair is that the omelet didn't come off."

As we gained the other side and turned into a part of Paris I did not know, he said, "We're almost at the Tribunal."

That gave me quite a queer feeling myself.

"Mercier is my *juge d'instruction*," Starr said. "He investigates my case. Then, if he is satisfied, he gives me a *non lieu*, that is, a paper signifying "no case," and that is the end of it. If he is *not* satisfied, he commits me to trial by court martial."

We had drawn up at a big barracks and one of the French soldiers on duty at the gate asked us our business. We were taken through into a courtyard and conducted to the foot of one of the staircases which led down into it, where there was some more business with another soldier seated at a table, and up a flight or two to a door.

When we got inside, a French soldier, tall, blond, very smart, rose and Starr introduced us. This was Captain Mercier.[1]

I produced the letter immediately from my handbag.

"You understand what this matter is about?" he asked in beautiful English. "Captain Starr was kept in slightly irregular circumstances while he was a prisoner at 84 Avenue Foch. That is why we are making this inquiry, which I hope he will be able to satisfy."

He took the letter, read it, passed it to his *greffier*, a *sous-officier* seated at the typewriter, and said, "Do you mind if we keep this to make a copy of it? We'll let you have it back later."

Starr explained our proposal to take him to the Avenue Foch and conduct him up onto the roofs.

"Certainly!" he said. "I shall be pleased to come."

We stayed talking for a little while; he was polite and considerate and certainly not unfriendly. As it was too late to go before lunch, it was agreed that we should depart now and return again at about two o'clock.

Starr was very pleased with what we had been able to arrange, and with the prospect of the whole thing being cleared up at last. "It's been awful for Michelle," he said.

---

[1] Now major (*commandant*).

After a moment he added, "I'm sorry for my brother too. People have said things to him, having heard them elsewhere, and it's not very nice for him. We haven't talked a great deal about this, but he said once that if I liked to tell him anything about it he'd be glad, just so that he'd know what to say to people."

As we drove back he went on, referring to the damaging talk in London, "I can't say it's done any harm to me. Michelle believes in me. It hasn't hurt me with the people I work with, or with anybody whose opinion I value. In that sense, you could say it doesn't matter at all! It's just *annoying*, really. When I think about it."

After lunch we went back to the Tribunal and collected Captain Mercier and his *greffier*. Mercier told Starr to drive us round by an interesting way, and at one point to stop the car, so that he could take us out to walk around the Place des Vosges to look at the architecture. This seemed to me a good sign; I felt he would hardly have taken us to show us beautiful things if he had really thought he was dealing with a traitor.

"Avenue Boche!" said Starr as we turned at last into the great, broad avenue of, for him, so many memories.

As we drew up to number 84, Mercier said, "Starr's castle!"

And as he went up to the door he mimicked the Germans, "*Schnell! Schnell!*"

So we made our way up the marble staircase to the landing where it came to an end at the door of the top maisonette.

The lady of the house let us in, showed us into what had been Kieffer's apartments, and then took us up a little white staircase to the fifth floor, which had been the scene of so much drama. I remember thinking how small everything was up here, and that with the German officials, and the guards, and the prisoners, there could not have been much room for anyone to move around. That staircase had an air as if it might have come out of a doll's house.

Starr took us into the guardroom and into Ernest's room, and showed what he meant by the impossibility of seeing anything that happened in the former in the mirror behind Ernest's head — though X and his specific accusations were never mentioned. Starr had become really alive now, even excited, darting here and there with great interest, in search of things he had known before, as keen as a terrier sniffing holes. I remember thinking that no man who had done something wrong here could possibly enjoy so much revisiting the scene where it had happened.

Some reconstruction had taken place, and he was for a moment put out to find a door in what had been one wall of his cell and a wall across what had been the passage from the guardroom to the cells and lavatory. Eventually we picked our way round, through what had been his first cell, where we had to step over a lot of lumber, to find the doors of "Madeleine's" and Faye's cells, which were locked, and then to the lavatory. Starr showed us the basin under which they had hidden the notes and the screwdriver, and we bent down and put our fingers into the crevice.

Somebody brought a key to "Madeleine's" cell, which was also filled with lumber; but we were unable to climb out onto the roofs, either through this cell or through Starr's, as nobody could find a pair of steps or anything adequate to climb on. In the end Starr suggested that we should go out, find the house at the back of the Avenue Foch through which they had come down, and go up through it onto the roofs that way.

So we went down again, and walked round into the Square du Bois de Boulogne. As we approached the house, Starr stopped short and exclaimed, "Look! They haven't even put a new pane in the window we broke!"

Sure enough, there was a window near the top, above a little ledge, filled in with corrugated iron.

We went up and rang the bell and the door was answered by a child. Mercier asked her if her mother was in. Just then a lady appeared.

Mercier said we had come to ask if we might go up through her house onto the roof, as we were interested in seeing the way some prisoners had taken.

She looked at Starr, examining his face for a moment very searchingly, and exclaimed, "Why, it was you who broke into my house one night during the war! You were sitting with a young lady on a couch in the room on the first floor when I came down and saw you. I asked you if you were thieves, and then I saw the lady was crying and realized that you must be prisoners who had escaped from the Avenue Foch."

She reproached him for not having told her at once who they were, declaring that she would have hidden them in a cupboard or somewhere. Starr said that it would have been quite useless, as the S.S., who knew they were in the building, would have searched it bit by bit until they found them, "even if they had had to take the floors up!" They argued the point for a couple of minutes.

Mercier, who had listened to this with a curious expression on his face, said to Starr aside, as we went up the stairs, "Well, I don't think there's any doubt that you were here, Starr!"

We got out onto the roof through a trap door, and were able to look across the courtyard at the back of 84 Avenue Foch, and to distinguish the different windows. We could also see the whole length of the roofs along which they had climbed although we could not go along them, as it would have meant getting up the wall down which they had come by means of the blanket rope.

We found the flower pots, or rather the remains of them, for they were completely smashed. Still hoping against hope, I insisted on poking about among fragments of earthenware, stirring through clots of earth, in search of some remnants of paper, until Mercier at last persuaded me that it was useless.

We had just settled once more into the car when Mercier got out and went back into a house at the entrance of the square. After a minute or two he rejoined us, saying, "You've got another witness, Starr. The *concierge du square* remembers you. I spoke with him. He was peeping from his window when the firing began, and saw the S.S. go into the other house and bring you out."

He had an appointment in the north of Paris and asked Starr to drive him and the *greffier* part of the way. Then, with thanks for the lift, they disappeared so quickly that Starr was quite unprepared for it. "Is that the end? Well, I suppose I'll be hearing from him."

He put me down at a point near my hotel.

"It's been quite an enjoyable day!" I said.

He gave me a queer smile. "It has, really, in its way. To think this could all have been done years ago!" I realized suddenly that he was terribly tired.

He gave me an appointment for the following evening, and we did some more work on the chapters of *Madeleine*. I also asked him to give me again some of the details of his rides with Kieffer's men, as I wanted to have them straight in case of any conversation about it with Miss Atkins. He did so, though he said he had put all this in the deposition which he made on his return to England; and, of course, he had told it all to Mercier.

"Well, what do you think yourself?" he asked me for the third time. "Now that you've heard all this and seen everything? Tell me honestly."

I met again two very straight and searching wide eyes. "I think you're all right," I said. "I believe everything you have told me."

3

Soon after I got back to London I wrote to Miss Atkins, telling her briefly that we had all been to the Avenue Foch, and (since I did not want to do things behind her back) mentioning that I had told Starr, as exactly as I could remember, everything she had said about him.

She asked me to dinner with her on Wednesday, the seventeenth of February. She gave me a cocktail first, and asked, "How's Bob?"

I had not the habit of thinking of Starr under his one-time code name, and looked at her inquiringly.

She said, "Starr! Has he been able to get another job yet?"

I did not immediately think of the reason why she asked this, and so replied, with genuine innocence, "I didn't know he'd ever been out of one. He's always had the same one, as far as I know. He took a day off for our visit to the Avenue Foch."

"Oh! He's carrying on, then?"

Then I remembered the message that he had received through the consulate: "Leave the country immediately." I said deliberately, "Of course he's staying there. He wouldn't dream of going away until this business is all cleared up."

"He *would* stay there!" she exclaimed. She paused, and then said, as if reflecting, "Yes. Knowing him, I know that he would stay."

I said, "It's all going very well. I think that at the Tribunal they're pretty satisfied."

"I expect they've got more important things to think about than Bob," she said. "His case is of so very little importance."

At dinner I asked her a question relative to an incident in "Madeleine's" career in the field. She looked surprised as she said, "You are rather changing the emphasis, aren't you? I thought it was to be mainly about her early life, as you knew her — with just a *little* about what happened after."

I replied that I had always wanted to make it as full as possible.

She said she thought people were no longer interested in books on the war, though they *were* interested to know what sort of people the women were who had been sent on Special Service, their motives, home life and previous background. She did not think there was any point in trying to establish the incidents of "Madeleine's" life in the field.

"It's rather an important part of her life!"

"I think the readers will find it much the least interesting part of your book," she retorted.

We had finished eating by now and returned to the armchairs by the fire, and she poured me a liqueur. "Why d'you want to see Ernest?" she asked me suddenly. I had mentioned that I was trying to get his address.

I was surprised that she should query something that

seemed to me so obvious. "Well, he arrested her! He would be able to tell me something about it."

"I think you would find, even if you did succeed in tracing him, that he was able to tell you very little of any interest. He was not a person of any importance at the Avenue Foch. He was not a brain. He would not, for instance, make a decision. He was the interpreter, and a jack-of-all-trades. He wouldn't have anything much to do with the interrogations. He would perhaps make a list of the prisoners' clothing when they came in. But he would hardly have anything to do with them afterwards."

I was astounded, for I was sure that she had spoken of him differently in November, when Vilayat and I had seen her together. But I said nothing — it seemed better to keep my counsel to myself. I said only that I should continue trying to find him, all the same.

The conversation had practically come to a standstill, and she asked me about my visit to the Avenue Foch.

Then I remembered that I wanted to talk about Starr; that I had come largely with the hope of making her see his case as I had come to see it by this time, and also of getting the answers to a couple of questions for him.

Finding it difficult to begin, I started off rather abruptly, "Starr would like to know whether it is permitted now to give real names corresponding to code names. His *juge d'instruction* asked him if he could tell him the real name of 'Henri,' and he would like to know if he has the right to give it."

"Oh, that!" she said, with a shade of impatience. "That doesn't matter at all."

"He can reveal it, then?"

"Yes."

"I like Starr," I said, "and I believe his story is true. Everything which it has been possible to check so far has proved to be correct, and besides that, I believe that his motives were what he says they were. I believe that he got himself into his position in the Avenue Foch in order to get information out, and that his loyalty was always to Britain."

She said very carefully, "He is not a *traitor.* . . . I told you at the beginning that he was not a traitor. He never gave any of our people to the Germans . . . or any of the French . . . and so far as I know he never gave the enemy any information either. Not that he'd much to give that I remember. He didn't betray anybody or anything . . . in that sense his conscience may be perfectly clear."

I was, of course, glad to hear this. It answered the question which I had promised Starr to ask. But I was puzzled by what seemed to me a change of attitude.

She noticed my expression and said, "But his position there was very undignified. Sitting right in the middle of the room where everybody had to see him as soon as they were brought in! It was a most upsetting spectacle for other prisoners. Why, he was the first vision they all had when they were brought up the stairs.[1] He lost his dignity."

I made some further attempt to put the thing as I saw it, but was conscious of not making any headway.

"I don't bear him any *animosity*," she said. "Don't think that. There's nothing personal in it. And I don't think he feels ill-used. I don't think he expected to be received with plaudits when he came back after that." After a moment she added, "Besides, there were some indefensible incidents. Absolutely indefensible." And she repeated, "He's a borderline case. That's what I told you from the beginning."

4

I went to Paris again just after Easter, and on April 17 Starr called for me in his car at my hotel early in the morning. He explained that his dog had been in a fight with another dog, and that he was taking it to the vet; but I could go along with him and we could talk on the way.

"Miss Atkins says you didn't give away any of our people, or any of the French, or, so far as she knows, any

---

[1] Starr says this is not quite correct. Only if they had been brought up from Fresnes or other prisons were the prisoners taken into the guardroom to wait till the interrogator was ready for them. Men who had been met on the field and brought straight back to the Avenue Foch were always taken into Ernest's room or another for interrogation and were not brought into the guardroom. Consequently, they did not see him (the door would be closed if a new prisoner was passing) until after the first session with the interrogator.

information," I said, almost the second I had got settled in the car.

His jaw nearly dropped. "In that case, what's it all about? I didn't think I did; but there seems to have been rather an atmosphere."

"She says you were very undignified!"

"I'd more important things to think about than my dignity. I was trying to stop more men from being sent to their death. Dignity was of no consequence."

Then he looked at me with a curious kind of smile, and said, "It's getting rather *less*, isn't it? First of all I was practically a traitor. Now just undignified. That's rather a diminution."

"She says there were indefensible incidents."

"What? When I took them pretending to look for a field for that plane, and so on?"

"But she said you didn't betray anyone and you could have a clear conscience in that sense."

"Well, what, then?"

He asked me if I had told her of our visit to the Avenue Foch with Mercier and that we had obtained confirmation of the attempt to escape.

"Yes. But that wasn't necessary for her. She's always said they knew that was true. It was Buckmaster who said they didn't. Buckmaster said they had only your word for it, and that was worth nothing."

Again there was a delayed reaction, almost none at first; but about five minutes afterwards, when the conversation had gone on to something else, he suddenly came out with, "Here, here, here! People can't just go around talking anyhow they like! There is such a thing as defamation."

He told me that when he had been at the Tribunal, Mercier had allowed him to see the statement Ernest had made concerning his conduct while he was a prisoner at the Avenue Foch, and had put it into his hand with the words, "It is *for* you. You can read what he wrote."

I told him that I was trying to obtain Ernest's address, and he said he knew an officer in the Sûreté who might perhaps be able to give it to me, and would try to arrange a meeting.

Just as we drew up at the vet's I told him of Miss Atkins's comment when I said that he was still in France to face the investigation: "Knowing him, I know that he would stay."

He was puzzled. "I should have thought that was a good way to be known, as somebody who wouldn't run away from a thing like that."

"I think it must be the first compliment you've ever had from them!"

He savored this, slowly. "The first compliment I've ever had from them!" And he chuckled.

The day after next, Wednesday, he phoned me early in the morning to say that he had been able to fix a rendezvous with his friend in the Sûreté for eleven-thirty in the Café Weber, near the Madeleine. I went, and found not one French officer, but two, and Starr.

We talked about the trial of the woman accused of the

betrayal of "Madeleine," Starr's affair, and other matters. The two French officers were pretty free in their comments on the organization of the French Section in London.

The one with whom Starr had made the appointment told us that at the end of the war they had succeeded only after great delay in getting access to the Germans from the Avenue Foch, who had been held by the British. Those of the Germans who had been taken to London said that they had been instructed there that they were not to "talk" when interrogated by the French. At first they had not done so; but later, when they had gained confidence, they had.

When the French had asked the British for Ernest, the reply came back that they had not got him, and did not know where he was. Yet, later, the French had had it confirmed that he was in British hands at the time when the French request for him was received.[1] Not until 1949 had they been able to have him for questioning.

Much of the information given by all these Germans would have been of greater interest if it could have been available earlier.

The French officer did not know the present address

[1] When I later met Ernest he told me that at the date in question he had been sent from the British internment camp at Staumüller back to the Americans, who had discharged him once already and asked him if he knew for what purpose he had been returned to them. As they had nothing they wanted to do with him, and as the British would not have him again, they sent him to the German (denazification) authorities. At a later period, wishing to be clear with everybody, he had put himself voluntarily at the disposition of the French.

of Ernest, and suggested I should ask Mercier. He thought all the Avenue Foch men, Ernest, Goetz, Placke, and the others, had gone back to Germany. Before we parted he gave me his name, and his telephone number in the Ministère de l'Intérieur.

Starr, who had shot me an occasional glance, was obviously well pleased with this interview. He said to me, "You see how much they distrust me! You see how careful they are what they say in front of a man who is being investigated!"

The following day I called at noon at the Tribunal Militaire to see Mercier. He gave me Ernest's address in Germany without making any difficulty. He said Ernest had been released in March with a *non lieu*.[1] "I don't see why he shouldn't tell you something about 'Madeleine,'" he said.

We talked a little more, and he walked with me to the Métro. "Let me give you a word of advice," he said. "You are writing about 'Madeleine.' Keep to the subject. It is more artistic. Remember that when you go to Germany — and everywhere." After a pause he went on, "Poor Starr! He knows too much. It is his tragedy."

Later in the day I was present at an interview between Mercier and Starr.

---

[1] Ernest received his *non lieu* after an eleven months' examination by the French. He was sent to Germany and told to report to the Service des Crimes de Guerre in Baden-Baden, where he was issued with a paper saying that he was *définitivement relâché*. As he had previously been examined by the American, British and German (denazification) authorities, he was now free.

The two men were standing. Mercier took out a packet of cigarettes and offered one to Starr.

"I wrote to Colonel Buckmaster some time ago," he said, "explained that we were making an investigation, and asked him if he would like to tell me anything about you. I have had no reply yet."

There was a moment's silence. I watched Starr and could feel him thinking what to say. He said, "I don't think you will."

Mercier did not reply quite instantaneously. It would be too much to say that he shot Starr a keen look; it was only a flicker; but in the seconds that elapsed I thought that he had taken in a number of things. Then he said simply, "It is not indispensable."

5

On my return from Germany in the summer I stopped for a day in Paris. Arriving in the early morning of June 27, I took my case to the hotel and then went straight to the Tribunal and tried to see Mercier. He was not in his office, but I got an appointment for four-thirty.

I then phoned Starr and he came out in the car to pick me up at the entrance, and took me to a café somewhere near.

I had a great deal to tell him. I had had confirmation of everything he had told me, and had also a lot of new things, some of them giving one to think.

"Ernest says that while he was at Staumüller he was

visited by a British N.C.O. from London, who tried to get him to make a statement against you."

Starr looked at me.

"Well, I don't mean 'tried' in the sense of using real pressure. But he put the questions in a way that prejudiced the answer. He said, 'He told you things, didn't he?' And Ernest said, 'No.' Then he said, 'But he had a great deal of personal liberty, and there must have been some reason why you allowed him so much.' Ernest said you didn't have a great deal of liberty; he never saw you go off the top floor without a guard. The N.C.O. went on, 'But he certainly had privileges that weren't allowed to other prisoners,' and Ernest said you didn't have any special privileges. This went on for quite a time. In the end Ernest wrote out a statement that was entirely 'for' you, and should have cleared you of all suspicions. He hoped it had. He asked me to give you his kind regards, and to say that he was very happy to learn that you were still alive."

He smiled at this a little.

I told him a great deal more and he let me get my story right off my chest. Only when I mentioned that I was going back to the Tribunal at four-thirty to see Mercier did he say casually, "By the way, I had a piece of paper from him this morning."

I looked up at him quickly.

"My *non lieu*. It came by the first post."

"I'm so glad!" I said, and meant it.

"It couldn't have been anything else."

The appointed time found me back in Mercier's office. He was more than half an hour late and the *greffier* entertained me with cigarettes and conversation. At length Mercier came in, with apologies, having had to accompany some prisoners out to Fresnes.

"Have you seen Starr?" he asked when we had exchanged greetings.

"Yes."

"Has he received something from us?"

"Yes."

"That was quick. It only went out yesterday afternoon."

He gave me a cigarette and then said slowly, threading his words as though he were choosing them with care, "I do believe that Starr is a very good, loyal and devoted Englishman. And he loves France, too."

III

The Decision to Publish

Neither starr nor I have wished to write a cynical or destructive book. "What good will it do if we tell all this?" was the chief question he raised when, in December 1952, I went to Issy-les-Moulineaux to ask his permission to write his story.

He was instantly taken with the idea; on the other hand, he did not want to publish anything that would be damaging to the country. We discussed it for several days before he gave his consent, and I could see that he was torn by contrary feelings. But none of the points he put up for consideration was self-regarding. Although deeply involved emotionally, he posed the problem on a level above that of personalities. "I'm trying to see this as though I weren't concerned in it. Is it for the good of the country that all this should be exposed? Will it do any good to anybody? That's the question we have to ask. It's the only one."

Again, speaking of the immense publicity that had been given to S.O.E. French Section, he said, "A lot of idealism has been worked up round certain personalities. Are we right to let all that down?"

But he really wanted the story to be written. Although

he was unable to help feeling bitter, his main concern was that the book should not be bitter. "I don't want *No. 13, Bob* to read like *Vengeance*," he said when he gave his consent.

I returned to Paris in February, and for the next five weeks we worked together practically every other evening.

The publication, in the latter part of January (just before I arrived in Paris), of *London Calling North Pole*, by H. J. Giskes, former chief of the German military counterespionage in Holland, revealing the deception through the radio sets of the Dutch Section of S.O.E., was an unexpected event, which we felt made matters easier for us. It took from us the heavy responsibility of being the first to tell the public that things of this kind happened.

Before *No. 13, Bob* had assumed its final form, my publishers sent me, for my interest, a book, *Monsieur Jean*, by Erich Borchers,[1] which proved to be the story of Hugo Bleicher, the Abwehr man who arrested Peter Churchill and Odette. In this I found a good deal about the game with the radio sets that was going on in France; it appeared that it was not only the Sicherheits Dienst which worked them back to London, but the Abwehr, too. The chapter heading "Weapons from Heaven"

[1] Published in 1951 by Adolf Sponholtz Verlag, Hanover. Since published in England by William Kimber under the title *Colonel Henri's Story*, translated and edited by Ian Colvin. My page references are to the German edition, and the quotations given are in my translation.

(*Waffen fallen von Himmel*) had an immediately familiar ring, and referred, in fact, to parachute drops
made in the Caen-Lisieux district, at Nantes and at
Limy. At Limy[1] Bleicher went himself to the field, "the
only German in a party of about twenty resolute and
brave French Resistance men to whom he appeared as
'the chief from London,' to receive a cargo of Sten guns,
hand grenades, dynamite," and so on. But the theme of
the radio sets that were worked back to London runs
throughout the book.

Borchers had some contact, too, with Kieffer, though
there was, in France as everywhere, some rivalry between
the Sicherheits Dienst and the Abwehr. Kieffer, he re-
marks,[2] was able to develop the radio game with London
to an extent never achieved by the Abwehr. He declares[3]
that by the end of November 1943 "hundreds of drops
were received every moon," and that "of the radios operating at that time, three quarters were in the hands of
the Gestapo." I do not know whether this statement is
correct; but the book makes unhappy reading.

Obviously, neither Starr nor I are in a position to get
at the figures of the cargoes or the lives lost. Starr can say
only what he saw and heard of what was going on while
he was a prisoner at the Avenue Foch. Only an inquiry at
a high level, with the exposure of papers inaccessible to
us, could hope to show the measure of our losses, while

[1] Pp. 108–109.
[2] P. 116.
[3] P. 124.

the appalling number of French deaths which followed from the mistakes through the radios would probably be impossible to estimate. We think it a pity that Colonel Buckmaster's book, *Specially Employed*, does not deal at all with the question of the radios that were worked back.

That Starr is a reliable witness I have had several occasions to verify. The last was very strange. My first book, *Madeleine*, appeared in its French translation at the end of April 1953, with the consequence that I received a letter from a Madame Marie-Madeleine Fourcade. She said she had read my book, and that she had been co-chief with Colonel Faye of the Resistance organization *L'Alliance*. For my interest, she enclosed an extraordinary document, a typescript copy of one of a number of manuscripts in the hand of Faye found, after his death, hidden in the cells he had occupied in the prisons of Bruchsal and Schwabische-Hall, Germany. She would let me see the original if I wished. It was an account of the escape which he, "Madeleine" and Starr had attempted to make from the Avenue Foch, and confirmed Starr's narrative, not only in the matter of the delay caused by "Madeleine's" failure to get her bar out, but even in such small points as the order in which the three of them walked along the roof carrying their blankets, Faye first, "Madeleine" in the middle and Starr bringing up the rear. And this was written within weeks of the event; Starr had told me the story after years. It said, as Starr had said, that the three of them had just gained the flat roofs opposite the back of 84 Avenue Foch when the airplanes came over, and that they all lay down to avoid being picked out by the beams of light. It told how they afterwards jumped up, made a second rope, and dropped to the level of the window which they broke, to enter the house through which they descended by the service staircase to the street, still keeping the same order. At the time when Starr was being investigated it would have been a capital document.

We have been careful to include in this book only what Starr is sure of. For this reason we have ventured no further than the presentation of the facts which are known to us; we have offered no theories to explain the mistakes which occurred, or the various unsatisfactory happenings to which we have been witness. This does not mean that we have no ideas ourselves, but we do not wish to impose them. We think that what we have done is to disclose a troubling situation, of which the English public should be aware.

As regards Starr's own affair, neither he nor I wish to accuse of malice those in London who have judged against him. We think simply that here, too, there has been a mistake.

IV

Microphones

AFTER THE MANUSCRIPT had been completed, with the exception of this chapter, I showed it, on the suggestion of my publishers and their lawyer, to a gentleman who had held senior officer's rank during the war and been in the London organizational side of S.O.E.; and he in his turn submitted it, as he later told me, to the Foreign Office.

Their reply, as he told me in an interview, was that they would not place any obstacles in the path of publication, if we were set on it, but that it would be likely to provoke the demand for a public inquiry, and "Starr will have to take what comes out in the wash." He had also informed, and consulted with, Miss Atkins and, I think, Colonel Buckmaster also. (I am not sure whether they actually read it; it was out of my hands over two months, from May 1 to July 8, the day of the interview.)

Summing up what he had gleaned from inquiries among the persons concerned (for he had no previous knowledge of Starr), he said, "Nobody doubts his basic loyalty; but the fact remains that he was a continual source of information for the Germans. There were concealed microphones in every room at the Avenue Foch, on all the time. You know that they can be installed very inconspicuously, on the undersides of pieces of furniture or camouflaged in the ornamentation." He pointed to a slightly prominent knob in the gilt molding over the mantelpiece. "*That* could be a microphone. There were *four in the guardroom.*"

No wonder they had been pleased to let Starr have little chats with other prisoners. "The old man, he never told." For a moment I wondered whom he was talking about. "Kieffer. He took the secret to the grave. He was a fighter. The war was never over for him. He wouldn't tell our people, when we had him for questioning. *The methods go on,*" he said meaningly. "A method can be used again. He knew that it could be used by his successors, if there should come another occasion. He took it to the *scaffold.*" He said this with a respect, and intensity, that was most impressive.

I was surprised Ernest had not told me. He said Ernest would not have known.

"If Kieffer didn't tell about the microphones, how did our people discover them?" I asked after a moment.

"I don't know," he answered. "Perhaps they found them, if the Germans hadn't had time to dismantle them before leaving." To go back to Starr; the Germans had of course been able to listen in to all his conversations with other prisoners. These prisoners, including the wireless operators whose sets the Germans were working back to London, pleased to see an English face, had been unable to resist the temptation "to let down their hair to

Starr," and so unwittingly provided the Germans with much background information about their private lives, experiences in the field and so forth. It was this background information that the Avenue Foch men had been able to draw on when faced by demands from London for confirmation that it was their own operators who were still working back to them. London would say, "Give proof of your identity," and the Avenue Foch man would reply, for instance, "Between such-and-such dates I was living in such-and-such a place." This would be something which the captured operator had said to Starr, and which had been picked up by microphone and recorded. But London would accept it as evidence of the identity of their man. "So you have the ironic situation that it was Starr himself who made possible the situation that he deplores. He made it possible for the Germans to fool us."

As I did not answer immediately, he said, "But I'm afraid that rather knocks the bottom out of your book. If he were dead you could call it *The Unconscious Traitor*."

And as he still didn't get a reply, he went on, "You see, Starr was a key man in Kieffer's game, on account of his unfortunate capacity — doubtless unintentionally exercised — for drawing people out. Kieffer recognized that he had found in him a natural instrument, and set him where he would serve." It was felt in London, he went on, that Starr might have asked himself for what purpose he had been kept about the premises — "doing, as he says, nothing of any great utility apparently" — all that time. Did he think the Germans had kept him there for nothing? He might have put it to himself that his presence must have been serving some purpose of which he was unaware, and asked himself what it could be. If he had faced up to it in that way, he might have thought of microphones. He stood accused of conceit, in the sense of overconfidence in his summing up of the situation and of his ability to handle it. He had thought the Germans were fools, and that proved his lack of objectivity. They were brilliant men at the Avenue Foch. The cleverest you could find in Europe. "Kieffer had the subtlest mind possible to conceive." It was Starr's very character that he had been able to see and use: his optimism and cheerful confidence which made other prisoners feel like unburdening themselves to him. "He was outmaneuvered. He was outclassed without knowing it."

"Why didn't they tell him?" was my first question, when I found my tongue at last.

He rather shrugged the question off at first. "How could they? It was during the war."

"But the war was over. The war with Germany. I mean, when Starr returned to England from Mauthausen. Why didn't they tell him then? Starr *asked* Buckmaster if there was anything wrong, and he said there wasn't."

"It's not the sort of thing you can say. What could Buckmaster have said? You can't say to a man, 'You're a fool!' straight out, just like that."

"But you *can!*" I said. "Buckmaster could have said that perfectly well!"

"He was a dupe. You can't tell a man he's been a dupe."

"You can tell a person anything when it's necessary, and when it's what you think to be the explanation of something, and especially when he's asked."

"D'you want Buckmaster to have said, 'You've been a bloody fool, and men have been sent to their death because of you'?"

"Yes, if that's how he felt! Starr would have rather had it that way. He's quite a big enough man to take it."

"One couldn't have been sure of that, and Buckmaster would have found it difficult to say. One never knows how a man will take it. It would have been a great shock and very upsetting for Starr to know that he had been responsible for the death of other men. And Buckmaster was probably feeling too sick about the whole thing to be able to talk about it sympathetically."

"It would have been better if he had expressed himself, however forcibly. It would have avoided all these years of bitterness. Starr has spent so many hours of his life in going over the answers he gave to the Germans during the different interrogations, trying to see where he could have made a slip, if he had done."

"He's looking in the wrong place!" he said. "Tell him to go back in his mind over the conversations he had with his fellow prisoners when they were alone together. It's there, not in the interrogations."

"Why does he always have to hear things from me?"

My vis-à-vis said that, whatever I might think about it, the decision not to tell Starr had been meant to be kind. The matter had been discussed by responsible people, fully and maturely, at the time. Some had been of the opinion that there ought to be a court martial, but a softer counsel had prevailed. An inquiry had been made, and those responsible had come to the conclusion that Starr probably did not know of the existence of the microphones, and there had seemed nothing to be gained from having all the fuss of a court martial. "It was decided to give him the benefit of the doubt." There had been a policy of "let's forget it" on the part of those responsible in London; a will to "let bygones be bygones" that was perfectly genuine.

Starr had given his parole, he said, and, "according to the book," that was not supposed to be done by officers. (I presumed he referred to whatever book contained the rules governing their conduct.) Nobody, he said, had made an issue out of that, or wished to do so. It was perhaps rather an academic point. Starr had used his discretion. Only the unhappy fact was that his use of it had had results which he had not foreseen, and which were most regrettable. He had taken the line of least resistance. However, nobody wanted to rub it in.

"One can say, if you like, that the whole thing was just unfortunate," he went on. One was faced now with a group of persons whose characters and approach to things were such that they had reacted upon each other badly. Their temperaments had been opposed, and they had misunderstood and perhaps misjudged each other's motives. "You can say it was just unhappy all round."

People in London had had to listen until they got sick of it to complaints about Starr from other men, returning from captivity, who had been his fellow prisoners at the Avenue Foch. "There were people out for his blood! Two men asked for permission to keep their Colts when given their equipment back. They said they were going to shoot Starr! They said they had told him things while they were at the Avenue Foch, and a day or two later they found the Germans knew them. And they were keeping a round each for him. We had a job soothing them down.

"I'm sorry for your book," he said, when at last we rose to say good-by. "I don't see what's left of it that you can publish. You can't very well publish it as it is, without reference to what I've just told you, because then it will all come out in a public inquiry, and the only result will be to make Starr look a fool."

"I think Starr will be willing to have this conversation included in the book," I said.

From his reaction, I am sure he was genuinely surprised.

I said I should have to think over what he had told me. "The decision is with Starr now. My feeling is that he will still want the book published."

My feeling was not wrong. I wrote to Starr that day,

giving the whole of the morning's conversation as nearly as I could remember it, repeating the actual phrases that had been used on both sides.

I received by express post a mammoth reply; the first line read, "Please have it sent for publication immediately."

He did not believe the story about the microphones, and suspected a bluff to frighten us from publication. He thought it would be a very good thing if there were a public inquiry. It was not he who had to fear what might come out in the wash.

"I was *never* left alone for a single minute with any of the prisoners whose circuit was being used by the Jerries." When he had seen any of them they were always with Ernest, or Dr. Goetz, or another French- and English-speaking member of the Sicherheits Dienst, and he and his coprisoners would never have imagined any words they exchanged to be unheard.

With "Archambault," about whom I had specifically asked him in my letter, he had certainly had a little conversation, but never with the illusion of privacy. There had been Germans there. And with "Madeleine" he had never had anything that could be called conversation at all. Once she had said to him, "Carry on! You're doing a great job keeping people's spirits up. More than any prisoner I ever saw." That must be the longest thing she had ever said to him. Otherwise it was just "Hullo," or something like that. In all the times that he had seen her, he did not suppose that she could

have spoken more than forty words to him altogether. All their serious communications had been
written and passed through the lavatory.

Which room did they mean, when they said there
were four microphones in the guardroom? Because the
guardroom had been changed during the course of his
stay. When he was first there, the room in which he
was set to work was the guardroom and the one next
door to it was Ernest's office; but later Ernest's room had
been turned into the guardroom (and kept so to the end,
for Ernest moved to an office on a lower floor), and
during the day Starr was left in possession of the former
guardroom, in which he was henceforth *alone*. This
change was made in the late autumn of 1943, when the
radio game was at its height; how strange to separate
him from other prisoners, and stop what little possibility to talk there had been, at that moment, if Kieffer had
in fact been making use of him as was suggested.

Only in the late spring[1] of the following year were
two prisoners, Southgate and his wireless operator, put
in with him for a while, in the cell-workroom, because
they, too, both did odd handy jobs in the daytime. But
their radio did not work back to London. And in
any case they did not talk about what they had been
doing.

Otherwise, the only prisoner with whom he was ever
alone was John, on two occasions. The first was when

---

[1] According to Buckmaster's book, *Specially Employed*, Southgate
was arrested in April 1944.

John had just been brought in and was put in Starr's cell for the night. They had both been so conscious of the abnormality and probable intent of the proceeding that they had hardly dared to speak a word, feeling that everything they said was being listened to.

The second occasion was either at Christmas or the New Year, when Kieffer brought them together and carried in a tray with bottles of whisky and gin on it, had a glass with them and wished them the best of the season, and then went away, leaving them alone with it. Again, the situation had been so transparently dangerous that they had been most careful of their tongues. In any case, John's radio had never been found by the Germans; he had always refused to tell them where he had put it.

To go back to the first phase, when the room was the guardroom: had it not struck anybody that the guardroom was always full of *guards*, and therefore not a place where a prisoner would feel like "letting his hair down"?

The question whether there had or had not been microphones was, from Starr's point of view, immaterial, since no words had been spoken between him and any person which could have been of interest to the Germans if recorded. But even of their existence, at any rate in every room of the Avenue Foch building and permanently active, as alleged, he was dubious. He recalled the incident prior to the escape, during the time that John had occupied a cell next to his, the cells having a wall in common with the guardroom. "It is very curious that the Morse tappings on the wall never reached the sensitive ears of the micros, thus giving away our intention to escape, when I asked John to come with us by tapping in Morse from my cell to his, the intervening wall of which communicated with the guardroom, where there were allegedly *four* mikes installed! And once I was tapping to a fellow next door too audibly and I was told to stop or there would be trouble. Funny to stop what might have been an interesting communication in Morse, don't you think?"

If microphones had been used to pick up conversations between prisoners, he found it impossible to believe that Ernest, "the chief interrogator," would not have known about it, since he would have been the person best placed to use the information so obtained.

Kieffer knew neither French nor English. If he really had had microphones installed, and Ernest had not known about it, it could only have been to check up on the loyalty of his staff. Indeed, if he had had them put in every room of the building, that could have been the *sole* purpose, since prisoners were kept only on the fifth floor.

Apart from anything else, if this remark was to be taken literally, the imagination boggles at what would be involved in practical terms. To have all the microphones listened to all the time, even if on records, would have entailed an enormous staff and vast expense.

Moreover, it would have been a difficult secret to keep, with so many people a party to it.

Again, if these microphones had been so special that Kieffer had had to take their secret to the scaffold, it seemed impossible to understand that he should have left them behind when they vacated the premises, "which they did in no hurry, before the Allies got there." (This was a point that had already occurred to me, for Ernest had told me of the time and care they spent in going through all the papers and effects in the building, decided which to take with them, which to destroy, and which to leave.)

About the two men who said they wanted to kill him: a man who really wanted to that would just do it, not say, "Please may I keep a gun to kill Starr?" But it would help to force home a false accusation. Might he have the names of these two men, because he would like to be confronted with them?

If a man had given information to the Germans, and was afraid that his chiefs in London would discover how much they knew about his work, then it would be a good cover to say, "I said nothing to the Germans; but I did say such-and-such a thing to Starr, and it must have got back to them." Unfortunately, the Germans did not need microphones to gather much information.

Naturally, he reacted with strong emotion to the accusation that he had been responsible for the continued sending of men to their death, when in fact he had tried to prevent it. "It is fiendish. Supposing I had not been *sure?* Supposing I had believed this terrible thing? I could have reproached myself to the end of my days."

Even if he had been to blame in the way alleged, it would not absolve those in London from their responsibility. They had sent the men out in response to the false messages, and to make out that it was a prisoner's fault could not exonerate them.

Regarding the question of parole, he had never been informed that it was not allowed for officers to give it. They were not told anything about this. Certainly he had never been given any book of rules to read. In the job on which they were sent out it would clearly have been impracticable for them to abide by a fixed code of rules intended to govern the conduct of officers serving in the normal way. Doubtless that was why they were not presented with any such code. Practically everything was left to their discretion. The principle implicit in their training and briefing was *débrouilles-toi* — use your wits and manage as you can. "The fact that this matter was never mentioned would account for the number of our boys who gave their parole."

In his own case, even if he had known that it was against the rules to do so, he would still have given his word of honor to Kieffer, since in the special circumstances it was his only way of continuing to serve. The important thing was that he should stay at the Avenue Foch, since only by remaining there could he hope to find a way to let London know that the radio sets were controlled by the Germans, and so to prevent further men from being sent out to meet their deaths. If he had refused to give his word it was most unlikely that Kieffer would have allowed him to stay, and he would have been placed beyond the possibility of action. Between obedience to a rule — a rule not designed to fit the circumstances — and the attempt to save men's lives, there could be no question of the choice.

I now wrote to the officer in London who had acted as intermediary between the Foreign Office and myself, putting practically all Starr's points and some of my own. I said that while it was obvious, in the event of an inquiry, that the whole thing might come down to a question of Starr's word or some other man's, it was my opinion that anyone who challenged Starr's account of what happened at the Avenue Foch would be on dangerous ground. I had known him now for almost four years, and had always found him a very reliable witness. More than once, chance had brought me the opportunity of checking statements he had made at a time when there seemed no possibility of proving them, and always I had found confirmation.

The letter I received in reply was longish, but did not attempt to deal in detail with any of Starr's points. The greater part of it consisted of a series of questions, put into the mouth of what seemed to be a prosecuting counsel, concerning Starr's position at the Avenue Foch, with which he might be confronted should the matter come into a court. This part ended, in quotes, "May

I suggest, Captain, that when you met Miss Overton Fuller you at last began to feel ill-used? . . . That your sound instinct to let sleeping dogs lie began to lose its wisdom? And who, in fact, ever accused you of being a traitor? I suggest, Captain Starr, that somebody should have done so — ten years ago, instead of giving you the benefit of the doubt." Here the quotes came to an end.

The last paragraph ran: "You know, I see him coming out of this a lot dirtier than he is now. Have you asked him to what extent he is actually suffering from the cloud which has so long drifted out of sight below the horizon? How many people at this moment, before you reveal the incalculable future by public searchlight, even know that that cloud was ever shadowing him? You and I, Buckmaster, Vera Atkins and two other people in the French Section — one or two Foreign Office men whom I have had to involve lately. Look closely at your motive. To help Starr? You cannot have any other. Will this help him? . . . I am thinking of his interest, of his happiness, of your heavy, heavy responsibility in his life. I say you must think very carefully. Send Starr this letter if you like."

I sent Starr a copy. He took a bad view of it, and regarded it as almost tantamount to an attempt at intimidation. At any rate, it seemed to both of us that there was in London a reluctance to our book's coming out, and we thought it came from fear of an inquiry. But in an attempt to create better relations, I wrote to Starr that I felt the signatory honestly believed what he wrote.

One thing appeared to us both as we studied the document: microphones had entirely vanished from the picture. Somehow we fancied we should not hear of them again.

What came over me now, as the result of all this, was the feeling, stronger than I had had it before, that Starr had been right in his deduction that he had been made the subject of false report in London, probably, as he said, by those who had something to hide.

From Ernest I had gathered that the greater number of prisoners had given things away, in varying degrees. Bitterness and disillusion had been a factor. But in any case, he saw an all-important moral division between those who knew what they were doing and those who, visibly, did not. There were perfectly loyal men who just slipped a bit while obviously struggling to keep on the "straight and narrow," and to whom he could see no blame attaching. I felt convinced that it was a state of affairs not appreciated in London; indeed, from all that had been said to me, it would appear not to be recognized at all. But of course the people here had, like any others, feelings and a psychology to be taken into consideration. Granting that some of their networks had been successful, especially in the more southerly and mountainous regions — as, for instance, that down in the west-southwest organized by George Starr,

"Hilaire," which endured to the Invasion, and was able to play a part in the liberation of the country — granting all this, one must suppose the people in London were distressed at what happened to those whose story is told here; and that they cast round for explanations. One could suppose that they took a pride in the men and women whom they sent out; and it would obviously be less painful to think there was one black sheep in an otherwise snowy flock than to see the greater part of the flock as having shown up, in the hour of trial, in varying shades of gray. It was at this point that a scapegoat became a psychological necessity; and anybody having in his circumstances anything suggesting that he might fit the role would be gratefully seized on.

I am not suggesting this was deliberate policy; I see it much more as a compulsive psychological need. As I said to Starr in a letter, I believed they were self-deceived in their estimate of him, rather than deceiving; and that one had to see not a devilishly cold Machiavellian plan, but a well-known psychological phenomenon; in short, the instinct — so deep that its promptings went unperceived, or nearly so, by the conscious mind — the instinct of every human creature who feels taxed with a fault to shift the blame for it onto something or someone felt to be outside the circle of those to be protected.

Starr's position at the table in the guardroom — "in the middle of the room" — had singled him out as a fit person for such a projection; and false reports from those whose word the authorities preferred — all centering on *him*, again because his position made him a target — had clinched the matter.

My own impression concerning those responsible in London — if I may give it without offense — is that they were the victims of an extraordinary obstinacy in sticking to judgments they had once made on people's characters, judgments highly emotional in their foundation, and in refusing to revise them. There was an absolutism about it, a refusal even to admit the possibility that they could be wrong (combined, however, with an inconsistency regarding the ground of complaint), which I had always noticed. One way or another, there had always to be something wrong with Starr, and if one ground were disposed of by logical argument then another was found to take its place. There was a fixation about it. And in this inflexibility there was also a conceit — far more frightening in its results than the conceit they accused Starr of.

They did not know who had served them well, and who ill.

In my opinion they were — as I had seen it in one or two instances — extraordinarily bad judges of character; though they all prided themselves on having a flair for summing up character. They had obviously miscalculated, for instance, the effect that the suggestion of a public inquiry would have on Starr and me. *They did not know whom they were dealing with*.

If they wanted Starr not to talk about what he knew,

they should have asked him. As he said to me, not once but many times, if, when he had met them after the war, they had told him simply that they would appreciate his silence concerning the German use of the radio sets, he would never have breathed a word. But that was the one thing they had never thought of trying. They thought only in terms of tactics — how to prevent people from coming in contact with him and so hearing his story, how to ensure that they would not believe it even if they did meet him. They never for one moment understood that they had to do with a man of honor — honor and a considerable largeness of heart — who would have kept what he had seen at the Avenue Foch a closed book if they had only made an appeal. Even at the last, after the manuscript had been submitted to the Foreign Office and after all that had passed, if they had written him a decent letter, asking him "for the sake of the country" not to make these revelations, it would have weighed with him. I knew it at the time, and after the episode was closed he said so to me. Yet, anxious as they clearly were to turn us from publication, they had never thought of it. They had never thought of the one argument to which he would have been vulnerable. (It was the irony of the situation that that was always the strongest thing with him.)

With me similarly. They could in safety have told me the truth, right at the beginning or as it became necessary, and I would have kept their confidence, instead of maneuvering all the time in the attempt to prevent me from finding out, a procedure which could only set me against them as I became aware of it. In plainest language, they created "enemies" where they need not have had them; or to put it another way — since neither Starr nor I really like the word "enemies" — by their oblique tactics they created in us a will that the truth should be exposed.

Naïveté which may leave one at the mercy of unscrupulous persons is perhaps a failing, especially on the part of those holding responsible positions; but failure to recognize decency, and equivocation when the greater safety would lie in frankness can, even from a practical point of view, be equally a blunder.